WORKSHOP 6
by and for teachers

THE TEACHER
AS WRITER

edited by
Maureen Barbieri and Linda Rief

HEINEMANN
Portsmouth, New Hampshire

Published by
Heinemann
A division of Reed Elsevier Inc.
361 Hanover Street   Portsmouth, NH 03801-3912
Offices and agents throughout the world

Every effort has been made to contact the copyright holders and students for permission to reprint borrowed material where necessary. We regret any oversights that may have occurred and would be happy to rectify them in future printings of this work.

The publisher is grateful to the following for permission to reprint previously published material:

Page 9: "Voice" by Mary Mercer Krogness was originally published in *Language Arts*, November 1986. Copyright 1986 by the National Council of Teachers of English. Reprinted with permission.

Pages 55-58: William Johnson's poem "Delivering Milk with Father" was first published in *Hiram Poetry Review* No. 48/49 (1990-91), pp. 41-45. Reprinted with permission.

Page 84: An excerpt from Linda Rief's chapter, "Writing for Life: Teacher and Students" was originally published in *Language Arts*, February 1994. Copyright 1994 by the National Council of Teachers of English.

Page 123: Ruth Whitman's poem "Spring" was first published in Norma Fox Mazer's *Waltzing on Water: Poetry by Women* by Dell Publishing.

ISBN 0-435-08816-5
ISSN 1043-1705

Design by Wladislaw Finne.

Printed in the United States of America on acid-free paper.
98 97 96 95 94 EB 5 4 3 2 1

CONTENTS

ABOUT
WORKSHOP 6

We've been friends for a long time. We came together in a research class at the University of New Hampshire, and we've stayed together through years of transition and turbulence. We share a common love of students, books, teaching, learning, and writing. No matter where we've taught, we've turned to each other with our concerns and questions about kids, with early drafts of writing, with successes and disappointments in our teaching, with discoveries of new authors. No one else lifts the other out of discouragement more quickly. No one else captures the essence of pure delight over a great book more empathetically. No one else responds to a draft of writing more honestly or more completely. We crowd the phone lines and the mails. We race to national conferences, in large part because they provide opportunities for face-to-face, all-night conversations. We have been friends for a long time.

So when Heinemann approached us with the idea of collaborating on the *Workshop* series, it took us no time to agree. The prospect of working together was too appealing, the notion of pulling together a whole book of teachers' writing too intoxicating, for us to seriously hesitate. Just as our own writing is central to our lives, we knew countless teachers for whom writing is equally sustaining, other teachers with whom we shared strong bonds. We have never met many of these teachers, but we've been invited into their classrooms and into their minds through their writing.

We knew teachers were writing more than academic articles, and we often talked about bringing this writing together in a book. "How do folks who don't write stay sane?" Tom Romano once asked, and we often wonder too. Teaching is a lonely profession. Despite the fact we are surrounded by 25 to 180 or more faces a day, we often feel alone. Writing not only helps us make sense of our lives and of the world, but writing, once published, lets us step *out* of our classrooms and talk with others. It nudges us beyond our closed classroom doors. It connects us to other people, people who care about what we are about, people with whom we need to share our questions, concerns, hopes, and fears. People who have come to writing with the desire to become better teachers have been surprised by what writing does for them personally.

These are the people who responded to our call for manuscripts for *Workshop 6*, people like Mike Steinberg, who struggles daily to make time for writing while meeting the increasing demands of his university students. Writing nourishes Mike's teaching and his life; he cannot do without it. Mike speaks for all of us when he says that serious writing at the expense of compassionate teaching isn't the issue. Teaching is a constant giving out to others rather than a giving back to ourselves. If writing empowers even a few of our students, then it certainly ought to empower us. Mary Pierce Brosmer reinforces that passion for teaching and writing. Writing allows us to "celebrate" our teaching lives, she says. Writing allows us to name our lives and professions "precious" and "worth singing." Writing gives us voice.

We thought of all the teachers we've met, through writing projects and in schools across the country, who know what Mike and Mary know, who somehow make the time to write not because they think they should but because they know they must. These are the teachers who write for themselves first because they have discovered the light that writing sheds on the rest of their work, on the rest of their lives.

Mary Mercer Krogness begins our book with her poem "Voice," which captures the essence of what we feel. Mary Pierce Brosmer writes out of the dilemmas of being mother/teacher/writer, and in so doing helps others recognize and value their own challenges and conflicts in these roles.

Bill Johnson, a published poet, shared "Delivering Milk with Father" with his seventh-grade social studies students and in the process showed them a powerful means of examining a memory. Linda Cunningham, in a course with Tom Romano, researched and wrote in a way that "produced an intensity and passion . . .

that made all that I learned part of me—how I feel, how I think, how I know what I know." How many of us can say that school research has changed our lives or the lives of our students?

Through poetry Richard Havenga looks more deeply into the "small things" that matter most to him. And Ellen Rennard celebrates Natalie Goldberg, one of her writing teachers and an author who has influenced many of our own attitudes about writing.

Larry Sipe and Jackie Murphy write fiction to explore the turbulent world of adolescence. In their stories we find ourselves and our students, and we become acutely aware that theirs is, more than ever, a fragile world.

For Sharon Lauer Miller, Lisa Siemens, Patricia McDonald-O'Brien, and Lisa Noble, writing and teaching connect implicitly and explicitly. Their teaching has grown more sensitive and more fruitful because they actively and regularly look for writing. Their stories remind us to be open with our students, allowing them to see us grappling with the messiness of the craft.

Kerry Ridolfi remembers that as a child her "best friend was a pen." Writing continues to be a mainstay in her life, as it is in her classroom. Looking back on a teacher who encouraged her, she reminds us how vital such respect can be for a child.

Continuing the *Workshop* tradition, we have included two interviews. Marcia Howell spoke with teacher-writer Susan Benedict and in *Workshop*'s "Teacher Interview" shares with us the story of another teacher who puts writing at the core of her classroom life. Bette Greene reveals in the "Author Interview" that she writes about what bothers her. Angry at injustice in the world, she challenges us to rethink our positions on important issues and helps us see yet another function of writing.

For us and for all of these teachers, writing is much more than a school endeavor. We do not write just to know what the students are going through, any more than they write solely to fulfill a classroom requirement. Writing is for real. We write not only to become more thoughtful teachers, we write to become more thoughtful human beings. We write for life.

Workshop 6 contributors, and all the other teachers who sent us stories, poems, and articles for consideration, understand this. It gives us optimism and hope to know that so many of us have set our sights in the same direction. Writing helps us understand why we do what we do. Writing brings us closer to our students. And writing connects us to one another. Readers of *Workshop* know this too, and we thank you for your part in our common vision. It is an honor to share this collection with you. Our hope is that it inspires other teachers to take their writing beyond their classrooms.

M.B. and L.R.

VOICE

"*S*peak up," the teacher said.
"We can't hear you."
"I've lost my voice," I gasped.

A serious thing
if you dream of wowing
the world with your
words.

But while I'm looking
for the voice that may be lost,
or reckoning with my voicelessness,
I'll let out random seams
to give myself a chance to grow
beyond the confines of a day;
to play with words, and let cool
breezes blow—
before I settle down

> to compress
> and distill,
> define
> and
> delete,
> pare down
> and
> bear down
> on this pencil.

Guest Essay
TEACHERS WRITING, WRITERS TEACHING: SERVING TWO PASSIONS

MICHAEL STEINBERG

*T*o write is to be transformed as a teacher of writing.

Janet Emig, 1989

Every summer for the past seven years, fifty to one hundred English teachers have gathered on the Northwestern Michigan College campus in Traverse City, on the shoreline of Lake Michigan. For six days and nights we live in dormitory rooms, take meals together, go to the beach, have cook-outs and poetry readings, and tour the surrounding area. But mostly we write and talk writing. Alums jokingly call us "The Traverse Bay Writing Camp for Teachers."

The first four mornings we write our own fiction, poetry, and personal essays. On the last day, like kindergartners, each group uses scissors, poster board, and crayons to create displays of the week's writing. By mid-morning, the walls are papered with teachers' poems, stories, plays. Every year this ritual evokes the same exhilaration and sadness—exhilaration because the writing is so personal, so powerful, and sadness because this liberating week is ending.

The Traverse Bay Workshop is a wonderfully playful interlude. As we share our discoveries and surprises, it feels like recess period on the school playground. We leave rejuvenated, promising each other, with the best of intentions, that we will continue to write and spend more time with our creative selves. But during the school year, it seems, that rarely happens. When

I run into those same teachers and ask how their writing is going, most sheepishly confess that they haven't written a line since the summer.

That's not an unusual scenario for English teachers. Last fall, en route to the National Council of Teachers of English Convention (NCTE), I saw many English teachers grading student papers; at my NCTE session a middle school teacher confessed she's been so busy teaching, attending committee meetings, and preparing students for statewide tests, she hasn't written in her journal for months. At that same convention I attended luncheons where teachers spoke with pride of their students' stories and poems, yet they never mentioned their own writing.

This dilemma has been troubling me ever since I became an English teacher. Most of us chose this profession because we love writing and teaching. But time and circumstance inevitably force us to choose one over the other, and the choosing isn't easy. When I'm writing regularly, the writing energizes my teaching. That's when I most enjoy being the facilitator and permission-giver for others who write. But the writing also steals time and energy. Before long student papers pile up and I fall behind in my preparation. Then I find myself rushing from my writing studio to classes, workshops, and committee meetings. By midterm I'm usually worn-down and frazzled.

But if I'm too busy—or if I deny myself the opportunity to write—I become irritable and edgy with my students. I scribble less-than-generous comments in the margins of their papers then feel guilty about what I said. It's then that I have to remind myself of what Donald Murray (1988) says: "I write because I need to write. I write because it's therapy for me. And I refuse to apologize or defend it."

That's good advice, but a lot of English teachers will agree instead with what Karen Jost (1990a) says in her provocative *English Journal* article, "Why High School English Teachers Should Not Write." Jost feels that "high school English teachers have little to gain professionally by writing" and that "writing is neither a realistic nor a professionally advantageous avocation" In addition, she writes:

> Our schedules certainly aren't conducive to making the effort. Besides our extra-classroom duties, most of us teach two or three different courses to 120 or more students daily. When we are not gasping under stacks of compositions or sharing a few holy minutes with our families and friends, you can often find us at basketball games, or chaperoning dances, or gritting our teeth through music concerts—

activities essential to the life of the school, the life we play an active role in. (66)

I want to resist Jost's argument, but I've been in enough public schools to know that most English/Language Arts teachers *are* overburdened. Jost also knows that writing takes time and discipline. "It is impossible," she notes, "to imagine commiting to 'serious' writing without sacrificing either our school extra-curricular involvement or our personal time" (1990a, 66).

I'm sure none of us would deny any of what Jost says. But "serious" writing at the expense of compassionate teaching isn't the issue. We can write to discover who we are, what we think, how we feel; we can write for our own growth and self-enrichment; we can take a few minutes a day and write just to blow off steam. In other words, our writing can serve as a brief leave from our teaching obligations; it can be our opportunity to be playful, to take some "safe" risks.

I noted some of these suggestions in a letter to Jost. I did not receive a reply, but her second *English Journal* article (Jost 1990b) gave me some idea of where her real passions lie. She writes

> Every now and then, I come across some kid, some back-row, C-average kid, who suddenly writes an essay that sings . . . or I look up from reading Shakespeare out loud one day and see someone who has that look—that arrested, flash of insight, I-can-hear-the-music-of-the-words look spread all over her face—or somebody shoves a battered notebook across my desk after class and asks in a half-embarrassed mumble if I would mind reading through one of his poems. These are the shooting stars that mark my way. (33)

A part of me admires, even envies, the Karen Josts of our profession. Married to their teaching, they seem more focused, more at peace than I'll ever be. But that's the dilemma I mentioned earlier. As satisfying as teaching can be, still it's a constant giving out to others rather than a giving back to ourselves. And it's precisely because we are always so concerned with enabling others to write that we should grant ourselves that same privilege. If writing can empower even a few of our students—as Karen Jost suggests it does—then it certainly ought to have a similar effect on us.

In 1986 I attended a presentation by Donald Graves, a session I wish all my colleagues could have experienced. With an evangelist's fervor and a Borscht Belt comedian's flair—his sparse hair flying in all directions, tie flapping over his right shoulder—Graves breezed through the room reciting a litany of reasons why English teachers should write: to model for our students what we teach, to help us understand their struggles to write, to realize what we're asking students to achieve. Heads nodded, fists pumped, but when Graves said, "Those are good reasons, but they're not good enough," everyone snapped to attention. "Sure we write because it makes us better teachers," he said. "Sure it helps us understand our students. But it's not just for the kids that we ought to do it. It's for ourselves. It's our outlet and our therapy. It's recess and play for big people. And, damn it, we need it more than they do."

Without pausing Graves invited us all to write for five to seven minutes. "Write anything you want to," he told us: "an observation, a poem, a meditation, whatever." We stumbled though the exercise, then he paired us with partners. Within minutes the room was alive with shared disclosures, with laughter, and with occasional tears. One teacher told me "this is the first time anybody has given me permission to write about myself."

Unfortunately, that's a sad fact of our teaching lives. Most of us became English teachers because writers and writing inspired us. But as we got more caught up in our professional and personal obligations, we let our original passions slip away.

I recall another speech I heard a few years ago at an NCTE convention. In his opening remarks, award-winning playwright and educator Mark Medoff (1988) told his audience, "I am thinking of the seductive business of immortality." Then he went on to praise a high school English teacher who encouraged him to become a writer but who recently took an early retirement. His teacher left the profession, Medoff said, not simply because of the numbers of students or papers to grade, nor because of increasing discipline problems. He retired because he believed that "he had stopped making a difference in the lives of his students."

Lamenting this, Medoff talked openly about his own falling away from teaching; about how seductive it was to think of renouncing the classroom and withdrawing to his study "to write my way to immortality." Curiously, what helped change Medoff's mind was a piece of his own writing, a play entitled *The Homage That Follows*. Katherine Samuels, the play's main character, is a dedicated English teacher who, like Medoff's own high school mentor, has burned out on teaching and has prematurely retired from the classroom. In a dream sequence the ghost of Samuel's newly-deceased daughter asks her teacher-mother, "When you were little what was your quintessential dream of what you'd accomplish when you grew up?" The mother replies, "I wanted to accomplish something for which homage would be paid. I wanted to perform so powerfully that people's very lives would be changed."

Medoff later informed us that at the end of his play he sends Katherine Samuels, renewed and re-energized, back to the classroom. I took Medoff's final comment to mean that the act of writing *The Homage That Follows* forced him, at least in part, to confront and to examine some of the reasons for his own falling away from teaching. He first had to change his own thinking about teaching before he could—with authentic passion and conviction—influence his students.

Whether or not my interpretation is accurate, Medoff's speech was a powerful message to those who believe English teaching is a calling. As teachers and learners we're all engaged in "the seductive business of immortality," the exploration of the enduring self. As such, we're constantly urging our students to write expressively, discover their own voices, mine their imaginations, write what they know best and feel most deeply about. We tell them writing is important for self-discovery and personal growth. Don't we owe it to ourselves, then, to find some time, even a few minutes, for our own writing? As Medoff said in closing, "We must all live for the surprises."

I became aware of those "surprises" in the mid-seventies, when I read Donald Murray's (1968) *A Writer Teaches Writing*. In that book, Murray urges English teachers to write along with their students, as well to write for their own self-discovery. Like most English teachers, I'd become overwhelmed with professional obligations and duties: teaching three composition classes plus overload courses, reading ninety student themes every few weeks, writing pseudo-scholarly articles in hopes of gaining tenure, attending after-class department meetings, presenting papers at the "right" professional conferences. I was doing everything but paying attention to what I loved most—the personal discoveries and surprises that came out of my own writing and reading, and the opportunity to share my learning with students. Those were, after all, the main reasons I'd become an English teacher.

I began searching and in time became aware of other teacher-writers: Stephen Tchudi writes books for teachers and creates adolescent fiction; Nancie Atwell runs her own school, leads teaching workshops, and writes books for teachers; Donald

Graves teaches, writes books for elementary teachers, and composes poetry. I could go on: Tom Romano, Linda Rief, Georgia Heard, Regie Routman, Shelley Harwayne, Carol Avery, Ralph Fletcher, Jack Wilde.

I'm not recommending all English teachers attempt to emulate these men and women, but I am acknowledging that they have shown me it's possible, though certainly not easy, to serve more than one passion.

At first my personal writing evolved slowly. I began by sharing my work with students and teaching writing workshops for public school teachers. A few years later I cofounded the Traverse Bay Summer Writing Workshops. In the meantime I rented a studio apartment where I wrote at night and on weekends. I began sending my work out, and within a year some small literary magazines had published a few of the personal essays I'd written at the Traverse Bay Workshop. At that same time I attended the Peninsula Writers' Summer Retreat, an annual gathering of Michigan teacher-writers. It was there I wrote my first poem. In the next few summers I went to the University of Iowa Writing Program and to the Aspen Writers' Conference, where I wrote plays, screenplays, and short stories. After some early jitters, I found I enjoyed being a student of writing, and I felt comfortable in the company of practicing writers.

As my confidence grew, I began reading my poems, essays, and stories at writing conferences, in classes, and at bookstores. Two years ago I created a small chapbook of poems, essays, and stories about growing up in New York in the fifties and sixties. Recently, two pieces from that collection won prizes and publication in national literary competitions. Despite the struggle and frustration inherent in writing and publishing, it all felt very satisfying. Satisfying in a different way from teaching.

In 1992–93 a sabbatical leave sandwiched between two cornea transplants allowed me sustained time off from teaching. So I enrolled in fiction, poetry, playwriting, and memoir writing classes. I attended class one or two nights a week, and spent my days and evenings writing. Originally, I'd thought this would be a kind of laid-back interlude, a leisurely break from teaching; a time to read and write a bit, walk the beach at my northern Michigan cottage; a chance to sit back and reflect, take inventory before I went back to the classroom. But that's not how it worked out. Some days I began writing in the early morning and when I finally looked up it had grown dark outside. Then there were days when composing one good paragraph felt like squeezing droplets of blood from my fingertips. Good days or bad, the writing became so absorbing I temporarily let go of my passion for teaching. A while back I tried to capture that feeling in a poem.

Writing Camp Heaven:
Glen Lake, 1987

From my deck I gaze out
over a blue/green lake
to green hills shaped like alligators.

Afternoon dawdles lazy,
a sleek tom napping in the sun.
I leaf through unread novels,
and begin to write: sketches and poems
I've imagined for years.

Sun melts away,
dips slowly below
the alligator's head
and I nod off.

In my sleeping/waking dream
the phone never rings
I meet no classes
hold no office hours
grade no papers
lead no workshops
attend no meetings.

I think I've died
and slipped quietly off
to writing camp heaven
where I gaze out
over a blue/green lake
to green hills shaped like alligators
and I read and write all day

For myself.

Before I returned to the classroom last fall I was worried that I'd lost my passion for teaching. Once I got back into teaching I was afraid my duties and obligations would diminish my writing time. At first that's exactly what happened. I couldn't focus on writing the way I could when I had all day to write. But I've since learned to write wherever and whenever I can fit it in. I've also learned to write for the joys and surprises, and for the sheer love of putting words on the page. Now when teaching and committee meetings and paper grading become a burden, the writing is my therapy.

These days I'm teaching full-time while completing the collection I began in 1991, finishing a coauthored teaching book, and writing a memoir. Moving between two worlds I've been thinking a lot about Mark Medoff's statement, "We are here to stimulate, by our imperfect example, others' growth. . . . This makes us better, fuller, more complete human beings." I hope the journey into my writing self has made me a "more complete human being," but I'm willing to settle for being a writing teacher who writes—who keeps trying to balance both passions, and who continues again and again to engage in "the seductive business of immortality."

References

Emig, Janet. 1989. Speech given at NCTE Spring Conference, April 9. Charleston, North Carolina.

Graves, Donald. 1986. Keynote address, "Focus on Writing Conference," November 10. Grand Rapids, Michigan.

Jost, Karen. 1990a. "Why High School Writing Teachers Should Not Write." *English Journal*, March, 65–66.

———. 1990b. "Why High School Writing Teachers Should Not Write, Revisited." *English Journal*, September, 32–33.

Medoff, Mark. 1988. Speech given at NCTE, March 28. Boston, Massachusetts.

Murray, Donald. 1968. *A Writer Teaches Writing*. Boston: Houghton Mifflin.

———. 1988. "Fluency: Planning for Surprise." Speech given at NCTE, November 29. St. Louis, Missouri.

Author Interview
WRITER AS TEACHER: LESSONS FROM BETTE GREENE

MAUREEN BARBIERI

*B*ette Greene is a fighter. Long committed to protesting injustice, she creates in her novels characters who struggle, suffer, and ultimately prevail as they stand up for their most deeply held beliefs. Listening to Greene describe her life as a writer is a bit like listening to Patty Bergen, feisty heroine of *Summer of My German Soldier* (Greene 1973), tell us why she behaves as she does. "I can't stand to see anyone brutalized," she exclaims earnestly, "no matter who it is. We have to speak out against the hatred in our society, and if we don't we are part of the problem."

Many people are familiar with Greene's adventure romances for younger readers, *Philip Hall Likes Me, I Reckon Maybe* and *Get On Out of Here, Philip Hall,* and with her novel *Them That Glitter and Them That Don't.* But it is *Summer of My German Soldier*— reprinted thirty-nine times in the Bantam edition alone—that has made the strongest impact on adolescents and their teachers.

Patty Bergen has stayed with many of us over the years. We care about her because she is smart and spunky and loyal. Patty is a person who loves words the way we do, and we love her for that too. She wrestles with a moral dilemma and finds the courage to live by her convictions. And she turns out to be Bette Greene.

"I grew up Jewish in the Bible Belt, down in Arkansas, and the Holocaust was a searing experience for me," Greene says. "Ruth, our housekeeper, was an important mentor. She was a woman with a lot of dignity, even though she was in a subservient position. She saw drama all around her, in people lining up to get their rations during the war, in everything. She helped me believe I could do anything; I learned so much from her."

Summer is largely autobiographical, Greene admits. "Our perception of what happened is more important than anything else. If you ask my sister about our childhood, she would have an entirely different story. I wrote this book in an attempt to understand my own life. We all do what we have to in order to survive."

Patty's surviving is important to me as a teacher of girls. Too often, when we ask a whole class to read the same novel, we worry about how the boys will react, believing the maxim that, "girls will read anything." The first year I taught, our booklist included *Johnny Tremain, A Day No Pigs Would Die, The Chocolate War, Tom Sawyer, Across Five Aprils, The Red Badge of Courage*, and *The Red Pony*. We forgot that our girls needed to find themselves in the literature too. And not just as heroines having boy-type adventures but as people struggling with issues of female adolescent development, the way Patty does. She wrestles with what Carol Gilligan (1982) calls her justice voice—"I am Jewish; as a German soldier, he has hurt my people"—and her care voice—"He is a human being, none of this is his fault, he is my friend." It is Patty's ambivalence and vulnerability that foster empathy in us, and, if we are female, validate the ways we make our own decisions.

In Carla Wayland, heroine of Greene's newest book, *The Drowning of Stephan Jones* (1991), we find another brave girl struggling with a moral issue. Her need to belong, to feel connected, to be in a relationship, supersedes, for a time, her need to be true to herself.

> I want everyone to like me! So what if once in a while I don't like or pretend to dislike people that I really like. What's the big deal? It's just that simple: I want to be liked. . . . There's nothing more important than being liked. (48)

Carla knows that harassing the gay couple, newly arrived in a neighboring town, is wrong, but she cannot bring herself to defy Andy; she wants too much to be his girlfriend. It is the same dilemma I have watched my students face again and again as they deal with dozens of moral choices, trying to figure out how to remain true to themselves and still stay close to those they care about.

> Carla felt as though the right side of her body was ripping itself away from the left and soon there would be two separate but equal halves. One of those halves wanted to defend the men because she really

liked them. She just felt they were nice, gentle people who didn't hurt others. In her heart, she knew that it was the right thing to do. But the other part of her wanted to stand by her man, no matter what damn fool thing he said or did. After all, suddenly she felt she belonged. She was Andy's girlfriend. Right or wrong, it was the womanly thing and loving thing to do since Andy would expect that behavior. Wouldn't that draw Andy and her that much closer together? Didn't she want to be a couple more than anything else? (Greene 1991, 58)

Katherine Paterson has said that reading is really rehearsal for living, and I like to think this was true of my students when they read *The Drowning of Stephan Jones*. What was difficult or impossible to see in themselves they saw clearly in Carla, writing comments in their logs such as:

• Carla should not be afraid to speak up. She should let people know her true feelings.
• Carla's mother is such a good role model. Carla should listen to her more.
• It's wrong for Carla to go along with what she knows is cruel and unfair.
• Lots of people joke about gays and make fun of them on TV and in the movies. I think it's wrong; it's a real problem. If a person is happy with who he is, we should respect that and leave him alone.

Bette Greene was moved to write about this "real problem" when she read a news story about the murder of a gay man. It incensed her to think that such violence was occurring across the country.

"I write about what haunts me," she says. "If I'm haunted, I know there is a good story there. And then I go and find the answer and in every case it's different. That's how I know it's a good story. I do stories that want to know the answer."

She researched hate crimes against gays all across the country, interviewing more than five hundred young men convicted of gay bashing and reviewing their case studies. Most saw nothing wrong in what they had done, believing that society in general and their clergymen in particular condone bigotry and violence against homosexuals. Greene's findings have led her to conclude that our schools are full of "designated victims," boys who prefer art and music and drama to football, boys who are slender, serious, scholarly, and sensitive. Gay or not, she insists, they are brutalized in schools.

"When you have a hate crime, you have to have hate," she says. "Where is all the hate in this country coming from? We're teaching it. It's coming from the pulpits of America and many of the coaches of America. And all students are affected by this bigotry—the victims, those who brutalize them, and those who stand by quietly and watch it happen."

Finding and writing stories is not new for Greene. Her first published piece appeared in the *Commercial Appeal*, a Memphis newspaper, when she was nine years old. She had witnessed a neighbor's barn burn and realized she had a tale to tell. Not only did the paper run her byline, but they also sent her a check for eighteen cents. "I decided then, it's a writer's life for me," she says.

But living a writer's life is not easy. Although *The Drowning of Stephan Jones* has received standing ovations and wide acclaim, it has also received criticism in some quarters for its treatment of organized religion. On several book promotion tours Greene has needed police protection in the face of death threats.

And there are more mundane problems. Even with all her experience, even with the raging success of her books, she was recently asked to write one hundred pages before being given an advance on a new novel. The publisher wants to be sure Bette Greene can "write adult."

"I don't relate to being successful," she insists. "It's always a struggle. I have a lot of doubts, but I keep going. The Greeks said that happiness is the pursuit of perfection; you work on it. If I have seven failures, I just keep thinking the eighth [attempt] will be okay. Nothing comes easily for me. I'm too lazy to do the work, and when I do the work, I'm too fearful to tell the truth because I'll get people mad at me. The laziness, the lack of discipline, and the fear of exposure are things I'm always in a battle with. It's a lot like a blind date. We want so much to be liked, but you can't be yourself and want to be liked. Needing to be liked curtails what I want to say. You should try to please yourself when you write."

Does she see herself as a teacher, trying to impart moral lessons? "I always hope people come away from reading my books feeling that they too have had that experience. That's what growing up is, having experiences and interpreting these experiences. And sometimes we can interpret them more wisely when they don't happen to us."

Certainly the conflicts in her novels cause readers, my own students among them, to reassess their attitudes. But as committed to social justice as she is, this is not Greene's conscious reason for writing. The best books, she believes, start with flesh and blood characters. The best books, the books that make readers think and feel and live differently, are written by authors who, through these characters, open themselves up to their own emotions.

"You work on it. You come to it. You learn to understand your life. In writing *Drowning*, I came to understand why my friend Jim had committed suicide when we were in high school. He was a designated victim, a creative young man who was labeled. Writing this brought that all back to me, all that pain. If someone cries over reading your book, it's because you cried first," she insists. "You can't make anyone feel anything you haven't felt."

Maya Angelou has said that teaching must be about loving. We are all, she believes, too afraid to use that word. I think of this when I think of Bette Greene's work, particularly *Summer of My German Soldier* and *The Drowning of Stephan Jones*. Greene is a writer who moves beyond her fears to share with readers what is in her heart. And in this sense, she is indeed a teacher. In her books we come face to face with human anguish, human turmoil, and human compassion. As Greene (1991) writes in *Drowning*: "Understanding someone else's pain may not be all there is to love, but surely it's got to be a part of love" (20).

References

Angelou, Maya. 1988. Speech at the National Council of Teachers of English Annual Convention.

Cormier, Robert. 1974. *The Chocolate War.* New York: Dell Publishing.

Crane, Stephen. 1964. *The Red Badge of Courage.* New York: Bantam Books.

Forbes, Esther. 1969. *Johnny Tremain.* New York: Dell Publishing.

Gilligan, Carol. 1982. *In a Different Voice: Psychological Theory and Women's Development.* Cambridge, MA, and London, England: Harvard University Press.

Greene, Bette. 1973. *Summer of My German Soldier.* New York: Bantam Books.

———. 1974. *Philip Hall Likes Me. I Reckon Maybe.* New York: Dell Publishing.

———. 1981. *Get On Out of Here, Philip Hall.* New York: Dell Publishing.

———. 1983. *Them That Glitter and Them That Don't.* New York: Random House Publishing.

———. 1991. *The Drowning of Stephan Jones.* New York: Bantam Books.

Hunt, Irene. 1964. *Across Five Aprils.* Chicago, IL: Follett Publishing Company.

Peck, Robert Newton. 1972. *A Day No Pigs Would Die.* New York: Dell Publishing.

Steinbeck, John. 1945. *The Red Pony.* New York: Viking Press.

Twain, Mark. 1979. *The Adventures of Tom Sawyer.* New York: Penguin Books, USA Inc.

Gillie Campbell of Newton, Massachusetts, contributed interview notes for this chapter. (April 1993, Brookline, MA)

HOW INFINITE IN POETRIES: CELEBRATING OURSELVES AS TEACHERS

MARY PIERCE BROSMER

As a teacher, I am always working toward the goal of creating space in which students will learn to pay attention—reverent attention—to their own lives and to the lives of those who are different from them. As a language teacher, I invite words from students that will "confer visibility" (Gibbons and Hahn 1989, 5) on their lives, provide opportunities to see themselves both as unique and as products of a complex set of social and political systems. Yet in striving to do this for students, I can easily ignore my own life, become invisible to myself. Madeleine Grumet, in *Bitter Milk* says "The maternal ethos of altruism, self-abnegation, and repetitive labor has denied the order and power of narrative to teachers, for to tell a story is to impose form on experience. Having relinquished our own beginnings, middles, and ends, our stories of teaching resemble soap operas whose narratives are also frequently interrupted, repetitive, and endless" (p. 87). During the holidays, when former students return telling their stories, I am keenly aware that I must continually create myself through my writing. As a teacher, at the end of my second decade of facilitating others' stories, others' self-creation, I know the crucial value of my continuing to grow, opening myself to possibilities, resisting the "fixedness" of life in schools: nonnegotiable time slots, standardized tests, curriculum requirements, and the like. (I have also become acutely aware of how few, and how frequently distorted, are the images of teachers and teaching in popular media and fiction. I believe that producing and publishing literature about teaching and teachers written *by* teachers is a very important political activity.)

24

As a poet, I have several favorite notions about what I hope my work is and does. From Adrienne Rich (1971), these words: "The moment of change is the only poem" (p. 49). I know that as I began to listen to myself in my poems, I began to change. I believe that individual growth and transformation effect systemic change, and that one approach to educational reform is through the writing and creativity of teachers. Another role of poetry is to "provoke mourning" (Gibbons and Hahn 1989, 6). Teachers, in our daily practice, encounter much that we must mourn if we are to preclude the diminished power that results from thwarted mourning. Finally, I believe that by writing poetry about our teaching lives we can celebrate these lives, name them precious and worth singing.

Midas of the New Right:
I receive a visit from a "concerned
citizen" and must listen to what he finds
offensive in a book I teach

I.
You are here, Mr. Midas,
in your bright suit,
your ears high under a new
barbering job.

Clean-shaven businessman,
elected official, church-goer.
When you begin by citing Christ
as your personal savior
the room smells and feels as if
someone has just told a dirty
joke, but no one is laughing.

You gouge innocent-in-themselves words
out of pages, leaving obscene holes
in the whole; at your touch
they begin to putrefy.
I am sickened by the sound of words
I have read or spoken so many times
with interest, delight, a chuckle
sickened by the sound of those same words
in your mouth.

II.
On my side of the table in this
civilized room where I am summoned
to hear your complaints, we begin

to fidget, feel sticky,
dream of going home to hot showers.

I am slow to speak,
fearful of what will happen to my
words when they are touched by
yours, already hanging in the air.

III.
I know I am being dragged by you
and those you have gathered to help,
armed by your citizens' rights,
dragged into the seedy backrooms
of your minds:
sour-smelling, ill-lit rooms
where pimply boys drool over
women's underwear pages
in Sears Roebuck catalogs,

dangerous rooms where older men
razor out pictures of parts of
women's bodies
and tape them to walls—
before moving on to other
   dismemberments.

IV.
I am growing desperate now,
I have to find a way out of this room
well-lit and respectable,
before you kick open the final door.

I will not be able to see you there,
but you will be—in the shadows
on your unmade bed.

I know what you will be doing
(as we all know, but are afraid to name
what you are doing even now under this
table where we sit to talk,)

prolonging it, prolonging it,
coming finally, fiercely

triumphantly shouting my name
my name
which turns to shit
in the memories of all the people
you've gathered here
to watch.

Slapping David Rose

I.

Right up front, I want to confess:
this is going to be a confessional poem.

Instead of digressing as I'm tempted
to do, temptation existing in a complicated
sequential relationship with sin itself
as I partially recall from my catechism,

(You see, I'm already digressing, to
avoid confessing,)

Let me just admit it:
my first year of teaching
I slapped an eleven-year-old child,
full across the face,
slapped an eleven-year-old child
while forty sixth-graders
in a hot classroom
at St. Philip the Apostle School
watched.

Not to worry, tongue-cluckers,
penance-prescribers,
my victim has worked
his vengeance on me
for decades now,

squirming up in his maroon sweater,
baggy at the shoulders,
his blonde hair plastered
in bowl-cut bangs to his pale forehead,
his freckles the only cheerful
thing about him,

everytime I speak about
what I've come to learn about teaching,
about classroom as community,
I see David Rose's face
still red with my handprint
after twenty years,
and my face colors
as though he'd slapped me—

II.

Oddly enough, that's what it felt like,
as though he slapped me,
day after day, watching me where I
stood under the crucifix

in that hot classroom
watching me,
and resisting, worse, scorning,
every word, every gesture,
every idea I created to teach,
to somehow reach him.

I don't even remember what it felt like—
the slapping—
it was over so fast,
it was as if my hand belonged to someone else,
as if I'd just watched a woman,
little more than a child herself,
slap a child
in a crowded classroom
in the foreign land
of inflicted cruelties

But, I remember, as if it happened
seconds ago in the most familiar
room of my life,
that David Rose, just sat there.
He resisted by not resisting,
he didn't move, didn't speak.

Then the oily smirk
of his victory over me
spread over his face,
and I stood there,
nailed to the spot
by forty pairs of eyes,
crucified, tasting
shame like the bitterest gall.

Year later, I understand enough
about power and its abuses, to wonder
what had brought David Rose to the place
where his only response to life was
no response.

I'll admit, however, that I still don't
understand enough about why
silence and resistance, and,
above all, smirking
provoke my fury,

I don't understand, why
I am, by nature or habit, the dark storm
swirling across cold, white
resistant surfaces

why I want to, and often do

fly in the faces
of pallid, wan, passive people.

Is it because I know
it is too dangerous to take them into my arms
that I take up arms against the armored,
the thick-shelled,
the shellacked,
the cynic,
the supercilious?

I cannot take them into my arms;
I know their coldness burns,
I've lost limbs,
parts I need,
through long,
sometimes even brief,
exposure
to the frozen.

IV.
God save me from the sullen,
the dead-eyed, the brittle-smiled child,
who, taught to hate,
taught me to hate him,
who, taught to fear,
taught me to fear him.

His freckles spread across
my dreams like disease,
I pray for him—
God save him
from teachers like me.

Woman: Writer/Teacher/Mother

*"It is humanly impossible for a woman who is a wife and mother
to work on a regular teaching job and write." (Tillie Olsen)*

I survive
like a garden in the city
squeezing up shoots and blooms
in sketchy rows: hollyhocks
hugging chain link fences,
sunflowers flattened against
the garage,
geraniums edging
the kitchen steps.

I imagine
a blanket of flowers sprayed

against rock walls, lavished
along highways, but I settle
for a handkerchief, folded
and hemmed, tucked in a pocket.

I labor
to push back the boundaries
wedge pale runners through the gridlock,
raising flowers in the crevices

Writing in the Margins.

References

Gibbons, Reginald, and Susan Hahn, eds. 1989. *Writing and Well-Being: Tri-Quarterly Magazine.* Evanston, IL: Northwestern University Press.

Grumet, Madeleine R. 1988. *Bitter Milk: Women and Teaching.* Amherst, Massachusetts: The University of Massachusetts Press.

Rich, Adrienne. 1971. *The Will To Change, Poems 1968–1970.* New York: W.W. Norton & Co.

A TEACHER WRITES TO FIND HER WAY

SHARON LAUER MILLER

I can't say that doing my own writing has given me all the right answers, but it has given me many good questions. For years I taught writing the way I'd learned it—the five-paragraph expository essay with supporting details. There was the descriptive paragraph, the persuasive paragraph, the narrative paragraph and, of course, the implication that none of these modes intermingled, which made no sense to either me or my students. As far as I knew, my own teachers never wrote. They corrected writing; therefore, I corrected writing. And they certainly never asked to watch me write. The way they taught writing, and consequently so did I, was more like teaching math, but because I didn't write, that realization hadn't occurred to me. There were glitches in this method, yes, but for the most part I was content with it.

Then my blissful ignorance was shattered. While teaching American literature and composition at a two-year college, I sometimes substitute taught a friend's eighth-grade class. Her middle school students were such an enjoyable departure from my college students. I usually brought something to read during free periods, but on this day, for some reason, I hadn't. I was sitting at Debbie's desk when my eyes caught a bright blue book called *In the Middle* (Atwell 1986). I carefully pulled it out from the other books on the shelf and met, for the first time, the warm smile of Nancie Atwell as she worked with her students. She was not in front of them, she was *with* them, and they looked like they were having a good time. I poured over the book every spare minute of that day.

When I began teaching my own class of seventh graders the next fall, I decided to try this new approach. What could be more pleasant than reading and writing with kids, especially if you could justify it as a more effective method than the traditional one? I believed everything I read about a process writing approach and whole language theory and was ready to put it all into practice—all except that one little part about the importance of the teacher's being a writer. I mean, let's be honest. It sounds great in an ideal world, but in reality too many teachers are too busy "correcting things" to do their own writing, and if they actually encouraged their students to write—well then, they'd have even *more* to correct.

In my heart I sincerely wanted to change as a teacher of reading and writing and believed that I could teach reading and writing in this new way without being a writer myself. Surely I could change everything else, follow every prescribed detail but that one minor one and still succeed. What I'd failed to realize was that I had to know what *I* was doing to be able to help my students. As a reading teacher, I was already there. I had long been a reader. I read constantly and voraciously, and my students knew that through the letters I wrote in their reading logs. I was teaching reading in a new way, as a reader. But the writing wasn't clicking.

I wasn't teaching writing the old, comfortable way I knew— talking about thesis and transition and supporting detail. I wasn't handing out topics and saying, "Go home and write about this and bring it back on Friday." I was following the "new" way *to the letter*. We opened every writing lab with a status-of-the-class report (Atwell 1986). We had occasional mini-lessons on technical problems in the students' work. I encouraged the students to confer with one another, and I made the rounds conferring with them. The students read parts of their work at the end of each class, and I encouraged specific response. We were all enthused, they were all writing willingly, but it still wasn't right, and I knew it. I just didn't know why.

If anyone asked, I said everything was going great. My students were coming up with their own topics and I was watching them write. But in truth I knew that I was more an innocent bystander than a guide. I longed for the safety of the old ways, where I was in charge and could honestly say I knew something about what I was teaching. As the year went on, things got more and more out of hand as problems arose that I, as a nonwriter, couldn't handle. Students were either abandoning their work out of frustration or were writing such lengthy papers that I couldn't keep up with reading them. Oh, for neat rows of seated students and short, assigned topics and deadlines and grades. Oh, for the order of the old world!

But the old world was not the real world; the real world is messy, and only people who know how to *do* can even begin to clean up the mess. Luckily, I somehow made it through that first year, found new enthusiasm, and rebounded the next year determined to do better. Unfortunately, I still hadn't realized that doing my own writing might allay my frustration and that of my students. Denial is a powerful wall.

This is where fate stepped in, and just in time. If I wasn't going to listen, then they were just going to speak louder. A new teacher arrived at my school—a teacher who taught process writing, a teacher who would be my friend and mentor. She was also a teacher who wrote. And she assumed that I wrote! In less than a month she'd organized an after-school writing group for teachers. Well, there I was, one of the few teachers in the school claiming to use the process approach, and I was going to tell her that I didn't write? Hardly!

So I forced myself to put my thoughts on paper, to keep a journal, to look for ideas to develop, to share my writing with a small response group of other teachers and painfully made it through the year. The only thing that kept me writing was the shame I felt when I brought nothing to share with my colleagues. I was rusty. It felt awkward and unsafe. I hated doing something in front of others that I didn't do well. It didn't occur to me then that my students felt the same way. I wasn't alert enough to see that yet.

One day while thumbing through my notebook filled with ideas for teaching, titles of books to read, and the like, I came upon a question I'd written the summer before on the way home from Williamsburg: why had I spent my entire visit there pining for my garden? The question still haunted me, so I decided to write an essay about it. Through the process of writing, I discovered an answer. I wasn't just plodding through, fleshing out an outline for someone else to see what I already knew. By the end of the essay, even I was astounded by its conclusion.

Remembering Grandpa Mike

Several years ago, on a trip to Williamsburg, a question hit me for which I had no answer. Seeing Williamsburg was something I had always wanted to do, and there I was—over thirty and finally there.

Williamsburg was, of course, fantastic. I really felt transported walking through the dusty streets, smoothing my hands over the worn stones of its little cemetery, eating Yorkshire pudding at the King's Tavern. Yet, every day as I wandered around Williamsburg with my husband and children, I was aware that I longed to get back home to my garden. It was August, and it was warm, and it was rainy, and my garden was growing—without me. My foxglove was blooming, my morning glories were climbing, my scarlet runner beans were getting fat. And I was in Williamsburg, miserable that I was missing it all.

The question that hit me was, why? It struck me that a week away from my garden should not cause me anxiety, especially when I was somewhere I had always wanted to be. And yet I was feeling anxious, almost like I did when I first had to leave my children when they were small. So why do I feel this strong connection to my garden?

My most recent gardening mentor has probably been Grandpa Mike, my husband's grandfather. A tall, gentle man of German descent, he immediately won my heart when I learned what an avid gardener he was. When Mark and I were first married, Grandpa Mike would faithfully send me clippings from *Organic Gardener*, and when we went to visit he'd give me packs of seeds from his hardware store to try. At family dinners, when everyone else was discussing investment banking or politics, Grandpa Mike would invite me to the attic to see how high the tomato plants in his makeshift greenhouse were. At Passover, we would go to a bed outside his kitchen door with my daughter, Rachel, and my son, Zachary, to dig up fresh horseradish for the seder—horseradish which now grows in my garden hundreds of miles away. Fifteen years ago, Grandpa Mike gave us a potted red geranium for our little apartment's garden which we still have today. It is woody and sort of "bonsaied," but it means more to me than any newly started leafy shoot ever could.

Oddly enough, it is that woody old geranium that has helped me to answer the question that has haunted me since Williamsburg. Grandpa Mike died this summer and, as we expected, Grandma Sadie reluctantly moved from their stately brick house to a neatly appointed retirement home. Added to my sadness for Grandma Sadie was the sadness I felt for Grandpa's abandoned gardens. I thought of the raised vegetable beds that he had built when he was ninety and the last flats of tomatoes that he had carefully tended during his last winter that were never planted in the spring. Who would care for his rosebushes or separate his horseradish? . . .

. . . we drove by the house just to see. From a block away, the huge industrial sign hit us—"For sale: zoned for office or apts."

. . . When we got back home that night, I began the laundry as I always did after such trips. When I got to the bottom of the basement steps, something caught my eye that sidetracked me from the waiting laundry. There hung Grandpa Mike's geranium, its roots bare, upside down on a rafter nail, supposedly in hibernation like all those lined up on either side of it. That part was normal; my geraniums hang that way every winter. But on this day what caught my eye was a red flower that had somehow pulled enough energy from Grandpa's sleeping plant to bloom.

I carefully broke it off and took it upstairs to my kitchen where I sat it in a dented, silver baby cup of water and put it on the windowsill above the sink. It was not a pale, sorry winter misfit, but a full, red mid-August blossom. I looked at it and knew the answer to my question from Williamsburg: the act of growing things connects me with life, and keeping things growing keeps people alive. This spring, and every spring, when we dig up our horseradish from the garden to place on our seder plate, we will remember Grandpa Mike.

This essay on gardening was my departure—a departure from writing out of obligation and a departure from the process I'd used for nearly twenty years because it was the only one I knew. It was also my first baby step toward becoming a teacher who knew how to teach writing by doing the only thing that can make that process clear—writing!

Of course, I didn't change my methodology drastically or overnight; my experience with the gardening essay was a departure, not a revelation. But I did begin to apply that experience to my teaching as I wrote more and more. Before, when students asked if they could read on a day scheduled for writing, I had said no, worrying that they would not write enough. As I began to notice my own writing habits, however, I realized that people don't always feel like writing on demand. But, clearly, kids who are excited about writing will write and can be trusted to do it on their own schedules. Wasn't I writing whenever I got the chance, now that I felt the need to?

Then, too, long before I wrote I had begun to see that I was wrong to have abandoned deadlines when I abandoned assigned work. Without deadlines, some students started ten different pieces in a term but finished none; others worked diligently on one long piece for which they could not see an end. Frustrated by this as I was, it was only when I faced my own writing deadlines that I could actually see their effect on a writer's work. Sure, I have written many first drafts in a burst of passion at midnight, but it was the knowledge that they needed to be finished for a reading or for publication that motivated me to complete them.

The problem of helping my students to find ideas for their writing was even more dramatically informed by my own writing. True, I had dutifully copied the suggested ideas from the appen-

dix of *In the Middle* and hung them on the classroom wall, but I
may as well have said, "I don't have a clue about how to help you
find a topic you care about because I never think about that sort
of thing myself." I was still thinking like a nonwriter. Once I
began to write regularly, though, I came to see how off base I
had been about the way writing is generated. Again, the gardening essay gave me my first clue. It was a piece I wrote out of
need—a need to know something about myself. It told me that
ideas come from inside the writer. I now realized that I had been
approaching writing from the outside in rather than from the
inside out. I had been treating my students like children who
couldn't decide what flavor of ice cream they wanted, and so I
read them the list. "Do you want chocolate, vanilla, or rocky
road? Do you want to write a short story, a poem, or an essay?"
Genuine as those questions may be in intent, they can't begin to
help a student discover what she wants to write about, or more
importantly, why she wants to write. Virginia Woolf (1973) said
that the idea for a book grew heavy in her mind "like a ripe pear:
pendant, gravid, asking to be cut or it will fall." I understood
this intellectually when I read it, but only when I began writing
did I begin to understand it emotionally. I came to see that ideas
grow inside a writer almost like a fetus and that as they are
nurtured and grow, the center of gravity these ideas develop
necessitates their birth. I began to understand that my job with
my students was not to help them come up with topics—that was
really just perpetuating the traditional "assigned topic paper" in
disguise—but rather to help them hear what they are thinking
about and thus what they need to write about. By sharing how I
listen to my own thoughts and find the center of gravity of those
thoughts, I teach my students how to listen to themselves and to
hear what they really care about. Frankly, my students need my
help much less now; as they finish a piece, they are not starting
at the beginning again as they were before. Now they know from
experience that one piece leads to another. There is no way that
I could have understood or taught this process without having
experienced it myself.

The most dramatic example of how my teaching of writing is
informed by my own writing occurred just recently. For the past
two years I've written poetry almost exclusively, having found
myself choosing this genre more and more often and recognizing
that it intrigues and fulfills me. Naturally, I have shared my
experience with my students and encouraged them to try poetry.
It's no wonder that they love it because they see that I do. When

I began to teach poetry, my students were intrigued with rhyme. While I wanted to expose them gently to free verse, both as readers and as writers, I didn't want to discourage their love of rhyme or imply that using rhyme was wrong or unsophisticated. So for two years I watched my students pass around the rhyming dictionaries I had bought for the classroom. This year I came upon an interview of poet Arnold Adoff (1988), which I decided to share with my sixth graders at the beginning of an intensive eight-week study of poetry.

> When I am drafting a poem, I visualize myself surfing—only I don't surf, but I'm kind of doing so on a word processor or on a sheet of paper. That's the way kids should be gliding into the process of revision—not sweating and grinding, attempting to find a word that rhymes at the end of a line that could be in any way close to what they really want to say. (p. 588)

Here I had been watching my students thumb through rhyming dictionaries every day without its having occurred to me that I didn't even own one at home! I hadn't been attending carefully enough to my own habits as a poet. But when I did, the poet in me said, "Arnold, you're absolutely right! I never use a rhyming dictionary and my poems are full of rhyming words that just come out because they want to be together." Three years ago, as a teacher who didn't write poetry, I would have read the article and responded, "Well, that sounds nice, but sixth graders love and need rhyming dictionaries." I would have had no way to test Adoff's opinion.

Of course, I shared my astonishment with my students. While I didn't forbid them to use rhyming dictionaries, I showed them in rough drafts of my own poems how internal rhymes—often whole sequences of them—just occurred without my consciously choosing them (see Figure 1). My students were intrigued by the idea of "surfing" through a draft of a poem first and then going back to see what rhymes had magically shown up. Now if a class member puts a poem on the board for us to help edit and we find one of those subtle, unintentional rhymes, someone will call out, "She's surfing." I predict that by next year my rhyming dictionaries will be permanently shelved.

Writing gives me an honest set of experiences from which I can truly help my students. What I tell them may not always work, but my words come from practice, not just from what I've heard works. Each year that I write, I learn more about being a writer; each year holds something new for me and my students. We listen together, we watch together, and we write—together!

Figure 1

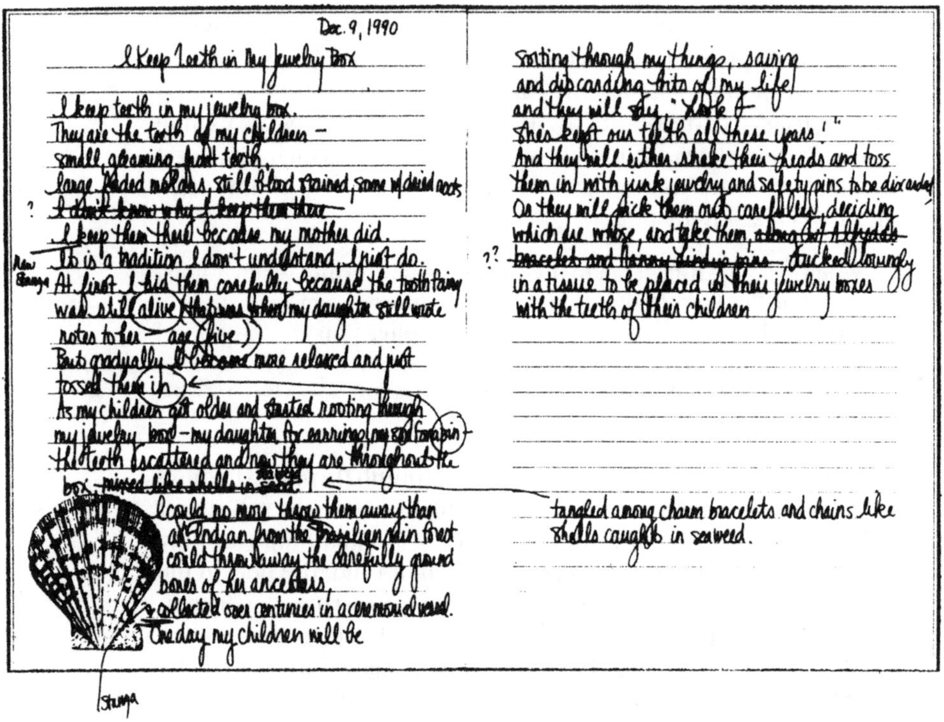
Dec. 9, 1990

I Keep Teeth in My Jewelry Box

I keep teeth in my jewelry box.
They are the teeth of my children –
small, gleaming front teeth,
large molars, still blood stained, some w/ dried roots
~~I don't know why I keep them there~~
I keep them there because my mother did.
It is a tradition I don't understand, I just do.
At first I hid them carefully because the tooth fairy
was still alive (that was when my daughter still wrote
notes to her – age (five))
But gradually I became more relaxed and just
tossed them in.
As my children got older and started rooting through
my jewelry box – my daughter for earrings, my son for a pin –
the teeth scattered and now they are throughout the
box, ~~mixed like shells in sand~~
I could no more throw them away than
an Indian from the Brazilian rain forest
could throw away the carefully ground
bones of her ancestors,
collected over centuries in a ceremonial vessel.
One day my children will be

sorting through my things, saving
and discarding bits of my life
and they will say, "Look
She's kept our teeth all these years!"
And they will either shake their heads and toss
them in with junk jewelry and safety pins to be discarded
Or they will pick them out carefully, deciding
which are whose, and take them, ~~along~~ ...
tucked lovingly
in a tissue to be placed in their jewelry boxes
with the teeth of their children

tangled among charm bracelets and chains like
shells caught in seaweed.

New Stanza

Stanza

References

Adoff, Arnold. 1988. "Profile: Arnold Adoff." *Language Arts*, 65: 584–590.

Atwell, Nancie. 1987. *In the Middle*. Portsmouth, NH: Boynton/Cook.

Woolf, Virginia. 1973. *A Writer's Diary: Being Extracts from the Diary of Virginia Woolf*. New York: Harcourt Brace Jovanovich.

SWEET SUMMER PRESERVES: WRITING ALL YEAR LONG

LISA SIEMENS

I am a teacher who happens also to be a writer. But for two short months each year, during the sun-drenched days of summer when I go to New Hampshire, I become a writer who also happens to be a teacher. This is not a mere play on words; the distinction is significant. Although I do write throughout the year, I often feel the writer in me being slowly smothered by the teacher, until it is squeezed into a space so small it can hardly breathe. From the first day of September until the last day of June, I live "school." Much of the time I write "school" as well. Each year, I wait for a kind of summer magic to cast its spell and change me back into the writer who spends two months searching for the parts of myself I have lost during the school year. I wait for July writing workshops and lazy August days to send me out to sea, pushing me into deeper water where I do more than just wade in an ocean of words and thoughts—where I swim.

After several years of despairing over how the lives of my students and the demands of school subsume my life, I have decided that I want to plunge headfirst into writing each day; I want to stop waiting for summer, because one of the problems with not swimming all winter is that it takes so long to get used to the water again.

This year I am trying to separate my school life from my other life by writing in two journals. One is filled with "school writing." This is a reflective journal in which I save precious moments, ask questions, occasionally wonder what school is all about, and frequently worry about what it is all about. This journal often takes me deeper into school than I care to go. So I have begun a second journal, a journal in which I do more than reflect on my students and my teaching. In this journal, I let writing lead me away from school. I explore different genres of writing—fiction, poetry, letters. This exploration usually takes the form of ten-minute "quick writes" that sometimes lead me places I never expected to go. I have also consciously decided to go beyond quick writes and work at the craft of writing—clarifying, refining, bringing certain pieces as near as possible to completion.

I know that there comes a time when my students' writing needs to leave the pages of their notebooks or the pockets of their writing folders. Whether a letter to a friend, a poem about ladybugs posted beside a jar crawling with the black-spotted insects, or a class-published book, my students all bring pieces to completion and share them with the public. Without occasional publication, these writers often wander aimlessly in their writing, never finding a strong focus, never taking a piece as far as it might go. I do the same thing. All writers need to go public at some point. I believe this is the element that has been missing from my winter writing.

This year I am determined to complete more pieces, and by some means, to send them out into the world. So far, this has meant writing many letters to friends and family and, yes, students too. (No matter how hard I try to separate the two sides of my life, the school world keeps sneaking into the pages of my "other" journal.) Included in these letters are drafts of poems I have written. When I send my poems to others I am finding an audience, and I know I will never find a safer audience than this. So far, I have received no rejection slips. On the contrary, each person has been thrilled to receive a poem no one else has ever seen.

I know that I will continue to be consumed by teaching and by my students' stories. I also know that writing can help me understand them better and even can lead me away from their stories to my own. I may be a teacher for ten months of the year, but I can also be a writer.

The World at Five

Great-grandma,
dressed in darkness
and wrapped in German,
sat at the edge of my

childhood like the hedges
shadowing my play.
On sun sprinkled days
I cradled my dolls
in Great-grandma's tulip quilts,
sang them to sleep
down streams of sidewalks,
and felt Great-grandma's
far away eyes lightly
rest upon my back.

Separated by miles of years
and yards of language,
we walked
in different worlds
until one day
walking through a windswept graveyard,
I saw her eyes clear
and blue studying
scratches in stone,
searching the weathered script
for her friends,
long ago girls
who once cradled
dolls in blankets,
sang them to sleep down
streams of sidewalks,
and stitched pink tulip quilts.

Driving home
clouds of German floated
softly around me
as sadness seeped into my eyes,
life settling silently
upon my five-year-old world.

China

The summer I was six
my mother said, "Go . . . dig for China."
Away I went spoon in hand,
a stainless-steel divining rod
guiding me to worlds unknown.

Away from golden days,
waving wheat,
and blush-pink poppies.
Slowly slipping
into darkened tunnels.
Silently

sifting the soil
for sunlight searching
for black-haired,
slant-eyed beauties.
Finding
                    dirt.
Reluctantly abandoning
hole after hole.
Grooming Grandma's green
and forever garden
into a field
of hope-filled hills.
Never doubting
China
waited
beneath
my feet.

"China" and "The World at Five" are both poems from my childhood. Although they were not written as a set, they certainly might have been. I cannot remember setting out to create the shadowy play between lightness and darkness, but it is there in both pieces. Both also began with strong images in my mind— one of me with a spoon digging, digging, digging; the other of my great-grandmother and I walking through a windy cemetery. Most of my poetry begins with strong pictures that seem to lie sleeping somewhere in my memory, waiting for some cue to awaken them. Once I begin writing, it can take many months to set the pictures to words.

"The World at Five" began as a quick write assignment that initially did not seem to work for me. In response to Mem Fox's, *Wilfred Gordon MacDonald Partridge*, I was to write about an elderly person I knew. After several blank minutes, I finally thought of my great-grandmother. I remembered walking with my grandma and my great-grandma through a graveyard, looking at stones engraved in German. I wrote: "Grandma Peters sat in the car, dressed in darkness, wisps of grey hair escaping from the roll coiled carefully each morning at the nape of her neck. I was five, she was seventy-five, separated by years and language. We were going down the road to the cemetery."

This entry sat in my journal, going nowhere, until several months later when I went with my grandmother to visit my grandfather's grave. While at the cemetary we stopped at Great-grandma's grave. I noticed that the years had not been kind to the German script engraved on the stone. Most of the letters had been eaten away by the wind and the rain. Seeing that stone and walking in the graveyard with my grandmother, who is now older than my great-grandmother was when we took that walk so many years ago, led me back to my journal entry. I thought about my childhood and about my great-grandmother. As a little girl my days were filled with color and sunshine, but Great-grandma Peters, always dressed in dark clothing, was never far away. Because we spoke different languages, we communicated little through words. The day we walked in the cemetery has stayed with me many years. I recall feeling unbearably sad that Great-grandma's friends had become little more than hard-to-read names on stones. It was probably the first time I realized that all people who died had once lived, had once skipped down sidewalks and played with dolls just as I did each day. Although the poem began as a memory of my great-grandmother, in the end it was more about a particular moment of my childhood—the moment I began to understand that life and death were part of the same thing.

"China" was a poem I never thought I would complete. Right from the start, I knew that it was about much more than a six-year-old digging in the garden. I began it during the dark days of March when my mood was equally dark. Truly, it began as a very dark poem, but I did not want it to be bleak. I wanted it to capture the optimism of childhood, the occasional doubts and dark thoughts of adulthood, and my belief that we are all searching for our own Chinas. Many times I abandoned it, the same way I abandoned those holes as a child. As winter turned to spring and spring to summer, the tone became brighter, the digging easier. By the time I completed it, this poem had traveled in more directions and gone through more revisions than anything else I have ever written. It has had a life of its own, and it has shown me that writing poetry is much like digging for China. Ultimately, the poem found its way into the hands of my mother, the person who first put a spoon in my hand and sent me out to dig.

Sweet Summer Preserves

I am saving a slice of summer—
hazy blue skies,
silky green shade,
and whispering leaves,
sealed in a jar

of Deep Creek water,
stored on my pantry shelf behind
pickled beets,
apple jelly,
and Grandma's strawberry jam.

On dark winter days,
when daylight brings
but a faint
fading of night,
while neighbors crunch
cornflakes and scowl at the sky,
I shall dine on toast
and sunshine.

And that is why
on this light
lazy day in July,
I am gathering all that I can
in a jar labeled
simply
SWEET SCENTED
SOUL SAVING
SUMMER PRESERVES.

Each August I visit my parents in the mountains. My days there are lazy ones, filled with books and talks and long, long walks. My favorite hike takes me two miles down the mountain to Deep Creek and a winding green walk to the bottom of a semisecret waterfall. I sit in the gorge, alone with the trees, the white sound of the falls, and my notebook. It is a perfect place and the perfect moment to be there.

One morning as I was madly scribbling in my notebook in an attempt to save the moment, I looked out of the gorge into the sky and had a feeling of being in a jar, the kind of quart sealer my grandmother had used for spicy crabapples. I floated in sun-splattered shadows, listening to the falls and the whispering aspens, the sky above sealing it all like a glass lid. The image was intense, as was the feeling. I felt rather like Leo Lionni's Frederick trying to save the colors and words of summer. Where I live on the snow-swept prairie, winter is colorless and I often feel that my words go dormant with the trees. So I worked on this poem, a taste of summer to get me through winter.

Knowing from the beginning that I wanted to work with the metaphor of a jar of preserves, I wrote the first section quickly. The words "I shall dine on toast and sunshine" also came easily, but I was not certain how to get to them, how best to capture winter's bleakness after summer's richness. I have pages of attempts at making this bridge. Most are rather wordy, some go in directions that take me nowhere. Although I did not do it consciously, I think that I described winter in as few words as possible to emphasize summer's abundance and not detract from the notion of the poem's being a jar of "sweet *summer* preserves." After I "finished" the poem I put it aside to see whether it would stand the test of time. All through September, whenever I read it, I changed words, playing with the cadence and flow, fine-tuning it until it captured the lightness and energy of a summer morning.

As I write these words, November's icy grayness is blurring my memory of August's brilliance. Most of my poems are tucked safely away in a file folder, but not this one. It is printed on sunshine yellow paper, never more than a glance away as I work at my computer. I wrote it first for myself, with purely practical reasons in mind. One quick peek and I am back at Deep Creek, breathing in the pine-soaked breeze, swirls of mountain air hushing the winter wind rattling at my windowpane.

Reference

Fox, Mem. 1985. *Wilfred Gordon McDonald Partridge*. Brooklyn, NY: Kane/Miller Book Publishers.

THE AMUSEMENT PARK

LAWRENCE SIPE

*N*ear the top of the roller coaster, I finally slip my hand in hers.

We look at each other's clasped hands, ignoring the clankety, rickety track and the pasteboard sign warning "Do not stand up" which frames the summit. As we pass under the sign, our eyes meet.

In her gaze, there is relief. After all, I have wasted a lot of time. I do not know what my eyes convey, but I do know what I feel: pure amazement that holding someone's hand could be so magical—and a shadow of fear that my crass adolescent obsession is showing through.

An instant later, we are part of a mechanical deathtrap which hurtles straight down toward the shallow muddy creek amid the groans of the wooden trestles, the bang-clang of the track, and the inevitable screams which trail like invisible ribbons through the rushing air. The rest of the ride is a blur, a nonevent, as I bask in the glow of self-congratulation.

For weeks, I have been scheming about this seventh-grade class trip to Hershey Park. Plotting my war-game strategies. Rehearsing my lines. What will I say? What will I wear? What will I do if Plan A fails? Does she really like me? Why am I such a coward? What different stuff is David Mann made of, that he can so effortlessly hold hands with Anita Long almost as soon as the bus lumbers out of the junior high school parking lot?

It has taken the bus ride, the long line to the admissions wicket, the bump cars, the ferris wheel, the petting zoo, and half the roller coaster, but never mind: I am on my way. I have achieved Objective One. I have held the hand of Debbie Lewis, and she has not pulled away or spit or screamed at me.

The roller coaster roars to a stop. In the car ahead, Richard Strickland and Robin Nichols are already stepping onto the platform. Dick is 4'5" and Robin is 5'6". They are "just friends." I think, I hope, that Debbie and I are just a few steps beyond this. In back of us, Dave has casually draped his arm around Anita's well-padded shoulders, his hand grazing tantalizingly close to paydirt. Just as casually, her hand works its way into his back pants pocket.

I close my eyes in sick envy. Rumor has it that they spend hours making out on her back porch, doing God knows what (and God knows how?) on the creaky porch swing.

Debbie and I do not talk much. I know she thinks I am "cute" because Ginny Wicks, an acne-covered blimp of a messenger, has hissed in my ear in the cafeteria line, maliciously feeding on my discomfort. But what does "cute" mean? A hamster is cute; a panda bear is cute. You do not make out with a panda bear or a hamster.

Our friendly sixsome proceeds to the Tilt-a-Whirl. Robin and Dick are having a great time; he saved her eyeglasses on the roller coaster, and the two are chattering away like squirrels. The rest of us do not talk: Anita and Dave because they are busy negotiating the crowded path as Siamese Twins; Debbie and I because we are trying to read each other's minds.

As we walk, my left arm receives an unexpected hypodermic of courage. I watch as it rises slowly and circles behind her pale blue shirt, the fingertips gingerly resting at the nape of her neck. The nerves in my wrist and forearm scream unbelieving signals to my fevered brain: through the thin cloth, I can actually feel her bra! This is almost too much too soon, but I swallow hard and look straight ahead. Debbie appears not to notice that a psychological revolution has just blown away thirteen years of my childhood in an instant.

The Tilt-a-Whirl is uneventful. We are strapped into separate compartments, like lunatics in metal straitjackets, so I cannot tell if Debbie shares Anita's interest in back pockets.

We stop for refreshment. Dave buys Anita a cherry snow cone, and they lick it together, their tanned cheeks brushing, their blonde hair tangling, their tongues lazily caressing the red ice chips as they exchange secret smiles. I buy a soda for Debbie and a hot dog for myself, hoping that meat will bring out the animal in me. Robin and Dick are giggling over an unwieldy mass of pink cotton candy.

The gypsy-gaudy carousel with its oompah music attracts us, and we board the swaying floor, two by two, the last passengers on the ark. There is an unoccupied double seat, carved like a swan; Dave and Anita claim it. Robin chooses a tiger; Dick a giraffe. Debbie and I mount side-by-side horses, mine white, hers black.

I try to ignore the up-and-down motion, for it suddenly occurs to me that every one of these rides has an erotic component. I am a creature of one idea; a single obsessive thought turns around and around in my head in time with the innocent carousel. Then Debbie stretches out her hand, and I grab it like a drowning sailor. We hold hands with difficulty as our horses lunge and rise in opposite directions. I have a second of self-consciousness about how absurd this must look, but it vanishes in a new wave of confidence.

After the carousel ride, Robin and Dick opt for the funhouse; perhaps the mirrors will even out their heights. But the rest of us are not here for fun. We are volunteer soldiers engaged on a dangerous and complicated mission: only the single-minded will survive. We do not want weird mirrors or huge rolling barrels or tilting floors. We want darkness, the sweet heart of darkness, which can be found in only one place.

The amusement called "Jungle Adventure" is a Freudian dream. Flat-bottomed, two-passenger boats are winched through a long, dark, watery tunnel. Dimly lit tableaux of monkeys, parrots, gorillas appear; the elephant's trunk jerks in front of us, then pulls away. Tarzan and a voluptuous Jane, wearing next to nothing, swing on the snakelike vines. The moist air fills with wild roars and mysterious screams.

In the boat ahead, oblivious to all these curiosities, Dave and Anita are busy having their own Jungle Adventure. In the hazy yellow light, legs and arms entwine, separate, entwine again. Wet, muffled groans languidly drift back to our virginal vessel. Some distance ahead, a grinding noise signals the ascent of the boats up a long incline to the open air, where, free from the winch, they will water ski to a splashdown climax.

Seconds are ticking. I know this is the last chance, the end of the line, the Normandy Invasion. I feel Debbie's impatience, exasperation. It is as palpable as the pounding in my chest.

I do not know who moves first. Our arms rise, collide, find

the right positions. I feel her breath on my cheek, the wisps of her long dark hair slide across my mouth, and then there is nothing but warm and wet and soft deliciousness. Our eyeglasses bump askew; our teeth collide and recoil; a strand of her hair tickles my nose. But none of this matters. I have kissed Debbie Lewis, and she has not pulled away or spit or screamed at me.

The boat races to its wet finish line in an avalanche of spray. As we stand beside each other, on dry land again, I am only a little surprised to feel her hand slide into my back pocket.

DAKOTA GRAIN: WRITING A MULTI-GENRE PAPER

LINDA CUNNINGHAM

She sat slumped in the alley
Like a half-empty sack of Dakota grain.
One hand curved loosely around an empty bottle of Jim
    Beam.
Fourteen, maybe fifteen
A kid in blue jeans and black braids
Senseless of dark or danger.

Like deer hunters with telescopic sights,
Officers on patrol spot her there in the alley
And close in on her.
She hears nothing: not the car, not their boots on asphalt,
Not the smash
Of glass
When they kick her empty bottle against the concrete
    wall.

"She's a goner, Bud. Won't wake up anytime soon.
Might's well take her to the tank
Before Ruby sees this Indian layin' around her
    laundromat."

Dumped half-conscious onto the back seat of the patrol
    car,
She tries to sit, falls back swearing
And slurring familiar syllables
"Goddam, Kanji—need five bucks, goddam."

The car moves through silent streets,
No lights or sirens; this business is routine.

50

At the jail the officers drag the boozy kid
Like a dressed venison out of the car
And into the cell at the back.
Her shoes drag along the painted concrete floor,
Rubber soles squeaking faintly.

They let her fall on the skimpy cot;
Big key clicks in the lock
And she cries weakly: "Kanji—need five bucks."
"Honey, I ain't your Kanji, and you don't need no five
    bucks.
But I do have somethin' here that you want.
Look at this, sweetheart; look at this!
Roll over now, honey; I like 'em to look at me."

Rough hands force open the snap on her jeans and yank
    them
Down, over young, muscled thighs and wobbly knees.
One small brown hand grabs at the air,
Reaching, finding nothing but the cold, hard metal
Of the sheriff's badge.
"Fuckin' Indian! Don't touch nothin' here!
You just lay still and take it—easy."

The tiny cot tips precariously.
His savage assault tears her body
And scars her soul
With rage
And shame
That will not fade.

Four violent thrusts and he shudders, satisfied.
"You want some, Bud?" he asks,
Sliding off the back end of the cot.

"Nope, maybe next time. Get your pants up;
I gotta get home."
"Suit yourself." Big key clanks in the lock again.
Echoes of footsteps fade down the hall
And she's alone.
Blue jeans crumpled in careless folds at her ankles,
Blood smeared on bare, trembling thighs.
Silent, muffled sobs "Kanji, Kanji . . ."

Outside the lock-up, dark, cold night.
"They love this, ya know. They're always askin' for it.
We done her a big favor.
She could of froze to death out here."

    The story of this poem is also the story of the writing model that helped produce it. The poem is one of fourteen original pieces I wrote in a creative writing course at Utah State University (USU). Inspired by Michael Ondaatje's (1974) *The Collected Works of Billy the Kid*, Tom Romano, a professor at USU, developed the multi-genre research paper as a writing model and has used it successfully in both high school and college classes. The multi-genre paper requires writing in a variety of genres on a subject of the writer's choice: a person, an era, or an event, for instance. Choosing a topic I was vitally interested in was crucial.

In 1991 I had read *Lakota Woman*, the autobiography of Mary Crow Dog (1991), and she'd been on my mind ever since. A feisty Sioux woman who came of age at the American Indian Movement standoff at Wounded Knee, South Dakota, in 1973, Mary Crow Dog and her story both repelled and attracted me. Her in-your-face attitude toward white American institutions and values left me defensive, but the spiritual power in the traditional Sioux ways fascinated me.

Early in the process I wrote "authority lists," or "idea lists," and lists of "pulls" to help identify areas I knew something about and felt drawn to. In *Lakota Woman* Mary Crow Dog notes that state police officers frequently arrested young Sioux women on drunk and disorderly charges (whether or not they were drunk) and then raped them. These assaults on young Sioux women weighed on my mind.

Weekly conferences with Tom helped keep me moving forward with the project, writing new pieces or significantly revising previously written material. In one conversation Tom noted that Mary Crow Dog's life was filled with brutalities; he encouraged me to try to capture some incidents with graphic description. The rapes of young Sioux girls by state troopers offered one obvious possibility.

These rapes, which Mary Crow Dog refers to in a general way in *Lakota Woman*, quickly coalesced in my mind into one concrete, imaginary incident. The ugliness of the assault as I imagined it drew me toward the condensed, powerful language that I think of as poetry, but having had no experience writing poetry, I was afraid to try it. I first wrote a short narrative, but it was limp and colorless. Risking utter failure, I then turned to free verse and produced a first draft in half an hour, fourteen hard-hitting lines—or so I thought:

> A drunk Indian girl
> Thirteen, fourteen years old
> Can't be left lying in alleys or
> On sidewalks—public places.

Officers
Cuff her, jail her for the night
Lead her stumbling to a cell
In the back
Where most won't see them
Pull dirty denim pants down her wobbling legs
Then mount her, one hand over her mouth
To muffle her weak crying.
"They love this. They're always asking for it.
Did you see how she wiggled her ass at me?"

I showed a copy to a colleague. He read it and laughed. My peer group suggested adding a touch of humor to lighten the tone. Both responses discouraged me, but both gave me important information—my intentions for the poem were not clear to readers.

When Tom reviewed the draft, he encouraged me to get "particular" in describing the girl and the scene to help readers establish a connection with her. I created a scenario in my mind, letting it play out like a movie. Using this visualization technique, I could freeze the scene and draw from a rich pool of details in setting and action. Then reading and analyzing Marge Piercy's poems helped me see how to craft the details using strong images, unexpected word choices, alliteration, and assonance.

By the fifth draft, my peer group no longer mistook the poem for a *light* piece. They could see my intent clearly, and they helped me clarify and focus lines that were still wobbly. Jim Mims, a group member, suggested the "fucking Indian" line for ironic twist—an important and appropriate addition. In fact, that word, with its current social connotations, captures the pervasive ruining of decent life for Native Americans.

The harder I worked on this poem, the more important it became to me. Ideas for revision distracted me from other writing I needed to do. I found it hard to stop fine-tuning; only the submission deadline was powerful enough to make me stop.

At the end of the USU course, a class member arranged for a group of drama students to read selected works from our papers. Four voices read this poem: a narrator, the two officers, and the girl. Their tense, dramatic reading laid bare the brutality of the rape. We all sat stunned for a moment.

Writing the multi-genre paper, particularly the rape poem, was the finest writing experience I have ever had. In addition to conferencing and peer response that really worked, the multi-genre model promoted successful writing by (1) allowing student-writers to choose topics we cared deeply about and (2) forc-ing us to know our subjects thoroughly in order to write in genres we hadn't tried. I have written many research papers and remained unchanged by the information I gathered, but writing the multi-genre paper created an intensity and passion about my subject that made all that I learned a part of me—how I feel, how I think, how I know what I know.

References

Crow Dog, Mary, and Richard Erdoes. 1991. *Lakota Woman.* New York: Harper Collins.
Ondaatje, Michael. 1974. *Billy the Kid.* New York: W. W. Norton & Co.

DELIVERING MILK WITH FATHER

WILLIAM JOHNSON

*T*hinking with head on pillow:
a full day's play
lost to work. All night
milk courses through
stainless steel pipes,
toward town, the soft glow
of dairy lights:
rows of sullen yellow trucks.

* *

At four a.m.
you feel as if
you watch yourself
get ready

then we sit
at the kitchen table:

the hum
of the refrigerator,
his veined hands
wrapped round
a white cup.

* *

Because a boy can't
easily be
broken, I walk,
hop, canter
down the gloomy
drives
of strangers;

carrying glass bottles,
they flare white
in the phosphorescent
glow
of outdoor light;
the smell of gas
in freshly mown
clumps of grass.
From the truck
he whispers . . .
"Watch you don't
bang them together!"

*   *

In full morning light
a young mother in a doorway
fresh open laughter,
intent on her list of items,
she closes her robe
and my eyes
to the dark circles
that press the easy fabric
of her dress.
I dawdle, holding
a great secret, then sail
down the drive
like a parachute of milkweed.

*   *

A kind of song:
the jangle of glass bottles
cold white milk
and the sound of the truck,
pulling, through the gears.

*   *

"Before the draft horse sale,
dreary hours of early morning
your grandfather would ready the horses
to the milk wagons.
Gentle clopping of hooves
down the brick streets of Warren,
impatient motorists
would damn near kill themselves."

*   *

The open mouth of a woman
waving sour buttermilk
beneath our faces.

He just stands there.

The lives of fathers
are altogether different
than their young sons imagine.
We share in common, the common hour,
the day suddenly emptied of form
. . . hiss, gasp a lawn sprinkler
continues its methodical rhythm.

              * *

Neighborhood boys and the smell of glove
   leather,
the simple, pious thwack of the bat;
me not there.

              * *

Throughout the day,
the chase,
a scarf of children
wavering
in the rearview mirror
trying to hail down
the truck,
shirtless boys with sweaty torsos
shy athletic girls
clamoring-up
the tall step
to breathlessly voice
orders
of fudgebars, popcicles, dreamcicles,
hands always careful
to count out the change.

              * *

Along a field
he pulls off
to catch-up
on statements.
The open door
and the swelling
till of cicadas,
late afternoon
of a common summer:
Father in milk uniform
cream, ice and sweat.

              * *

Father would always tell me
"You can't always get what you want"
but I never understood the place
in his voice; now I join him in
looking for gray milk boxes,

garages with smooth concrete floors;
we circulate past people's things,
bicycles, riding lawn mowers,
endless elaborate lawncare devices;
with evening setting in, other fathers
return home from work
waving, loosening their ties, taking the milk in;
then sometimes whole families would flow
out the door into their bright automobiles
perhaps already headed for dinner or a show
lives bridled with possibility.

* *

In the blue cusp
of an August evening,
windows down, our Belair hurtling us home;
Father in rakish lawlessness
opens a bottle of chocolate milk,
downs half, then hands the other half to me.

Work is sweet.

I am always amazed by what great webs our minds are, their capacity to snag so many raw bits of information. One morning, finding the house unusually quiet, bedroom windows wide open, I heard the faint sound of a truck pulling through the gears. The engine sounded the exact sequence of notes my father's milk truck had. This blue-collar music so deeply embedded in my mind brought back a flood of associations: milk bottles, cream, ice, and sweat, a virtual plumb line of associations that led back to days over twenty years ago. Sometimes I think we were meant to have more sumptuous summer mornings like this, where we let our memories select and make a film of our past. It would be better than TV!

I think "Delivering Milk" is mostly a poem about the rhythm of a workday. More than a father/son poem filled with the animation of quality time, this is a poem about sheer time, time spent between a father and son, when a boy realizes the full arc, the good and bad, of a father's day.

Later, I began to test the memories of my seventh-grade students. Could they write good poems and memoirs about their relatively short past? I found, of course, that they could. Exercises designed to unearth images from the past resulted in whole paragraphs of context, and my students too felt the health one gets by "winning meaning," marking in some way the endless fury of their days.

Teacher Interview
ENGAGED IN LEARNING: AN INTERVIEW WITH SUSAN BENEDICT

MARCIA HOWELL

Susan Benedict is a teacher, an author, an editor, and a listener. We met one clear, cold February day to talk about her teaching. She sat relaxed on her couch, blue eyes bright, chestnut-colored hair curling softly around her face. We sipped hot tea.

An interest in working with both students and teachers led Susan to Edgecomb, Maine, and Nancie Atwell's school, The Center for Teaching and Learning, a demonstration school where teams of teachers observe and learn. After working as a consultant and demonstration teacher in other schools and spending two summers teaching in the University of Massachusetts Writing Project, Susan prefers demonstration teaching in her own classroom. "One of the things that is really enjoyable about The Center is that it brings all of my past efforts together, but with the added benefit that the demonstration teaching is with my own students, not with children I don't know," she says.

Her early work focused on children's literacy development, which has remained a strong interest throughout her teaching career. Working with fifth and sixth graders at The Center, she has expanded her concept of literacy to include art, which she explores with her students in their language arts studies.

"The more possibilities that we can give kids, the more we can open things up, the greater the likelihood they're going to find their way and we're going to learn what they know," says Susan.

Her students investigate the potentialities of art and the connections between art and writing. They keep nature notebooks, an idea Susan learned from Joan Zelonis, in which they make weekly observations about the world around them: they draw what they observe, and they write about both their art and their observations. These notebooks then become tools for generating ideas and places to practice writing and drawing.

The person who nudged Susan toward this expansion into art was Karen Ernst (1993), author of *Picturing Learning*, who adapted Nancie Atwell's writing workshop model as the basis for a whole-school art program at her school in Connecticut. Having heard Karen speak at a conference, Susan started thinking about the connection between visual images and graphic representation in children's storytelling. She added a weekly artists' workshop to the daily writing workshop in order to open up the world of writing. By bringing art into the writing classroom, Susan created the possibility of art's leading to writing.

As one might expect of beginners, her students stuck with the safe and familiar—magic marker representations of expressionless, cartoonlike people; no perspective; little sense of proportion. Susan observes, "Sam and Nathaniel, for example, repeatedly drew the hulls of boats with a ruler and filled in the bottom of the paper with flat, blue water, then added an inch and a half of sky across the top."

Realizing that her students lacked the tools they needed, Susan determined to provide those tools. For several months she, another teacher, and a parent volunteer used class time to give mini-lessons in drawing objects, shading, perspective, and watercolor and torn paper techniques. Susan learned right along with her students. Once these techniques were in each student's "tool box," she returned to the workshop format with a challenge to her students: "Okay, now that you have more tools with which to work, tell me what you're going to do."

Last winter, Mary Beth Owens, illustrator and author of *A Caribou Alphabet*, was an artist-in-residence at The Center. Susan and her students prepared for the artist's visit by studying animals in the winter landscapes, which was to be the focus of Owens' residency. The students looked at winter landscapes noticing light and shadow, shape and perspective, and drew the scenes in their notebooks. Reflecting on the act of drawing, they wrote observations of the process. Through this observation and recording, Susan's students began to see more. Some found new insights in their writing, some in their drawing, some in both. Wonder and questioning followed their scrutiny. "Where did this block of wood come from? Where has it been? What are the stories it has to tell?" "They're theorizing poetically," Susan explains, "and also scientifically. I'm not sure if that's writing, if it's art, or if it's science. I'm interested in reading, writing, and graphic representation right across the curriculum."

A similar retooling occurred in Susan's writing workshop. Realizing that most of her students seemed to gain no ground when they were stuck in the familiar and predictable, she began reading and discussing published writers' work with her class. When her students write fiction, they examine a published fiction writer's work and ask, "What do fiction writers do?" Students bring the books they're reading into the writing workshop. Discussing Mildred Taylor's (1976) *Roll of Thunder, Hear My Cry*, for instance, they look at how Taylor handles the narrative voice and ask questions about the advantages of speaking through the central character, Cassie, as opposed to speaking through another character or an omniscient narrator. What implications do Taylor's choices have for their own writing?

In addition to looking at writers' techniques, Susan and her students examine what writers need to know in order to write. They talk about the kind of information Taylor needed to write about Cassie and her family and how she might have obtained it. What do students know about, and what do they need to find out? Susan shows her students how research helps her write not only nonfiction but also fiction and poetry. "You can't start writing without content, even if it's fiction," she says.

Last fall, poet Ralph Fletcher visited The Center. In anticipation of his visit, Susan and her students read many different poems to discover what poets write about and what conventions they use. After Fletcher had worked with the students and teachers for a day, Susan observed that they all began to show an incredible sensitivity to the possible poems that existed around them, waiting to be written.

If students are interested in a particular area of expertise but unsure of how to write about it, Susan brings magazine articles to class to demonstrate how nonfiction writers write. She tries to teach real-life writing instead of written-for-the-teacher/school-report writing.

For their science class, her students needed to write about their experiments with electricity. Susan was searching for a format the young scientists could use when a colleague gave her copies of a biologist's report that had been presented at a scholarly conference. Susan and her class read the report, examining how real scientists wrote about what they did and how they communicated with other scientists. That scientific paper became the model from which the students worked.

As well as using professional writing for inquiry and example in her classroom, Susan models her own writing. Although she doesn't write with her students in every writing workshop, she often starts pieces there, continues working on them outside the classroom, and brings back revisions to show her students. They see their teacher at work as a writer.

Although writing fiction and poetry does not come easily to her, she is not afraid to let students see her struggle. Last winter many of her students were writing fiction that she thought weak. Unsure of the best way to help them create more powerful stories, she finally decided to try writing fiction herself, a departure from her usual articles about teaching. On an overhead transparency, in front of her students, she started writing a story, letting them see her draw on her own experience, establish the narrative voice, experiment with flashbacks and transitions, and deal with covering a long period of time. Susan wanted her story to be as good as one of Cynthia Rylant's, whose writing she loves. "Of course it isn't even close," Susan said. Her story may not have become all that she'd wanted, but her students write better fiction now.

Susan strongly believes students need to see teachers at work in their field of expertise. They learn how to be scientists from observing science teachers working as scientists. Students need to work as much as possible like real-world scientists, historians, mathematicians, artists, musicians, and writers. "If students never see their teachers practicing their skills and their craft, it's hard for them to understand how they can begin to gain entry into that area of study," reasons Susan.

Working side by side with her students is an important aspect of Susan's teaching. Certainly she creates the tone and structure of her class, lays the foundation for classroom work, and teaches what she values, yet she also plunges into the nitty gritty of daily classroom tasks. She becomes a learner with her students. When she started the artists' workshop this past year, she didn't consider herself an artist. Some of her students were talented in art; others found it difficult. She drew, painted, and constructed with them. They saw her struggle to put onto paper what her eyes saw. Occasionally, a student would approach Susan, look at her work, and say, "Gee, Susan. . . ." She would reply, "I know." She wasn't an expert, but she could tell her students what she saw, and she could show them her battle to control her hands to get an image on the paper. She believes that seeing her engaged in learning gives her students confidence to try. "A teacher doesn't need to know all the answers, but boy, we've got to be in the trenches with our students or we don't understand what they're going through," she says.

The winter sun poured in the windows as we finished our talk and tea. I sipped one last time from the mug and, setting it on the table, read its inscription. "Reimagining School—Dare to Dream."

References

Ernst, Karen. 1993. *Picturing Learning: Artists and Writers in the Classroom.* Portsmouth, NH: Heinemann.

Owens, Mary B. 1988. *A Caribou Alphabet.* Gardiner, ME: Tilbury House.

Taylor, Mildred D. 1976. *Roll of Thunder, Hear My Cry.* New York: Dial Books.

A WINTER'S DUSK, A CHILD'S VOICE

PATRICIA McDONALD-O'BRIEN

Writing is life work, not desk work . . .

Lucy McCormick Calkins
Living Between the Lines

My husband Pat, our friends Mike and Cheryl, and I were all gussied up and heading out for dinner, but I had the wrong address for the White Dog Cafe. As we pulled up to the curb, a street man stood next to the parking meter, waiting for us to get out of the car. He peeked in the passenger window, talking to himself. I asked our friends in the back seat, "Does he look psychotic to you?"

"No! No! Just get out of the car and find the restaurant. It should be in the next block."

He introduced himself as Roland. Roland said he would watch the car for us, "'Cause nobody gets a ticket when Roland's watching." We gave him the prepared pocket change, pumped quarters into the meter, and searched for the restaurant.

For about ten minutes we walked around looking for any sign of the upscale cafe. We encountered two other street people, told them we had given our money to Roland, and tried not to make eye contact. I felt uneasy, wary, but I began to see. I noticed how I don't really look at "these" people . . . how I keep my distance both physically and emotionally. I was a visitor, a tourist, an intruder. It seemed we were from places more distant than the ten-mile drive into town could explain. I noticed how driving around this neighborhood was insulating—a windshield panorama of poverty—the six o'clock news version I "tsk-tsk" in my living room. But it was only as we walked these streets that I noticed the emptiness of locked doors, boarded windows . . . no chatty neighbors on stoops, no adolescents draped on the corner. I noticed brick and cement and traffic and tar. It appeared monochromatic—the men's voices, their children's faces, their layers of clothing, the winter's dusk. These men popped out of nowhere, like fish striking a line, and we dealt with one another as quickly as possible. After walking around in Roland's territory, we gave him a few bucks and a brief lecture on demon rum, then pulled away.

The following Monday morning, at the request of their teacher, I introduced a fifth-grade class to their first poetry workshop. As the school's reading specialist, I wasn't met with the cool breezes reserved for substitute teachers nor was I greeted with the warmth shown the career day athlete. All desks were cleared. The students were quiet and polite as I read poem after poem. I read poetry from overheads. I read poetry from handouts. I made sure to read poems about sports and about pretty new clothes. The students remained very still; the kinder ones smiled at me. At best, I was novel entertainment. At worst I was boring. A boy in the second row tried to balance the heel of his right sneaker on the toe of his left sneaker. I feared multiple requests for the restroom would commence soon. Where were those responses I'd read about in Heinemann books? Children swaying to poetic rhythms, swearing off rhyme, and loving Robert Frost? This just wasn't working. The room was too tense and too quiet. I was too tense and too noisy. I was forcing it. I now realize I wasn't inviting them into the verse. I hadn't asked for participation; I had asked for quiet attention and I was getting it! I was attempting to teach poetry as if it were a workbook page.

It was time to write. As an act of pure faith, I stood bravely before them and asked them to write their strongest feelings— a special birthday, a favorite pet, a best friend, even images of Grandma. I knew they had stories and images within them. Having anticipated an assignment, they asked the obligatory questions. "How long does it have to be?" "Does it have to rhyme?" "Can we write together?" I suggested that we write individually and "rhymelessly" for about ten minutes.

I sat at the back table with my notebook open, happy for some time to get off stage and regroup, reflect. I put my pen to paper, intending to write a few notes on how to improve the poetry workshop, when I discovered my thoughts returning to my Saturday night encounter with Roland. I began to write and lost track of time. Writing with other writers had steadied my nerves, and I knew I had the beginnings of a poem. When I finally came out from behind my desk, I dropped my role as "expert" and joined this community of fifth-grade writers. Just like Saturday night, I had to get out of the car and become one of "them" to even begin to get a sense of this neighborhood. Through my writing, I discovered how to develop my teaching.

However, I was still a visitor to this class. So with trepidation I approached a young man who introduced himself as Curtis. I asked him if he would listen to my rough draft, then entitled "Roland." He listened and nodded and finally said, "This is all about what you saw, what you did. Did Roland or those other guys move or say anything to you?" Impressed by his insight and grateful for his brevity, I thanked him and jotted his comments in the margins. Other students took the cue and began reading their drafts to one another. Three boys gathered on a windowsill and laughed as Bruno read his poem about a lunchtime table tennis game. The room filled with storytelling, some nervous giggling, and choruses of "Ya' wanna hear my poem?" Dark-haired Angela, her jaw set, stared at a blank piece of paper. Curtis had pulled his desk away from the group and, head down, immersed himself in writing. On my way out the door, I snooped over his shoulder and he told me he was writing about playing the piano. "Can I read it when you're finished?" I whispered as the teacher was diving into the next subject. "Yeah, sure, Ms. O'Brien."

For weeks, over the din in the hallway, I occasionally heard Curtis ask, "Is it done yet?" I responded hurriedly, "No, no, still at it, Curtis, still at it. Writing poetry is hard work ya' know!" No visible sympathy from Curtis.

"Roland" haunted me for months; it just wasn't right. Often when I began to write about something else, it would appear instead, just as had happened that first day in class. My colleagues grabbed coffee cups and patiently listened as I read them yet another version.

In April, Curtis's homeroom teacher rushed into my room exclaiming, "Have you seen this? Curtis wrote a poetry book! Isn't that great? It is dedicated to you: 'To Ms. O'Brien—she knows why.' Do you know what that means?"

Yes, it means I got out of the car and connected with another writer. It means that fifth graders and their teachers have poems to write. It means through sharing, we learn. And yes, Curtis, Roland did say something to me that January evening. He kept asking me for "Chicken Money."

Chicken Money

Brick row houses, locked twice
Giraffe-necked street lights
Pour milky puddles
Onto black tar
Framed by cement

Men move as video game villains
Blankets trail over rounded shoulders
Super hero capes
One pushes a silver shopping cart
Jammed with rags, newspapers, and his
Two small children
Peek at me through the bars

Roland lives on this corner,
38th and Chestnut.
Hustles, "Chicken money, c'mon man
I need some
Chicken money."

Feed him thirty-five cents
Hope he leaves me
Alone.

Feed the parking meter
Three dollars
Hope I don't get a ticket

For chicken scratch.

Reference

Calkins, Lucy McCormick. 1990. *Living Between the Lines.* Portsmouth, NH: Heinemann.

HOMEWARD

ELLEN RENNARD

Natalie, you visit me always unexpectedly,
in some city far from home, or
when I'm asleep
you knock on the door like room service,
and I stand, embarrassed in my rumpled nightshirt
as you bring in your box of well-used books.
You send me messages
through a medium;
you appear before me
like Hawthorne's ghost, Surveyor Pue
(though you would never point at me
but simply smile and say,
"Go!")

I traveled to the Garden Cafe
where you write.
Sitting on a wooden chair
the color of honey,
I ordered one of your
chocolate chip cookies
the size of a plate.
When you were in Japan,
I stayed at your house
in Santa Fe.
I slept in your bed,
drank tea at your table,
looked in your closet,

saw your leather jacket
and cowboy boots,
the long scarf with gold threads.
I thought, "Maybe if I buy new clothes,
give my suits to charity,
maybe then I could be
like Natalie."

You told me to start a writing group
and I did—
a gay priest,
a Zen bookseller,
an insurance agent,
and an English teacher.
We met at the Parkmoor,
sat in an orange booth, writing,
as Muzak played and waitresses banged dishes
in gray plastic bins.

When I returned from spring break
the priest said, "I've started a novel
about smoking cigars and playing billiards
in the basement with Uncle Lou."
The poets said, "We want to write alone,
but you can hear us read
at Page One."
After that we never met again.

It has been too long
since that winter around
the fire in Taos.

Yet there you are
in that picture I carry,
sitting beside me on an adobe wall,
your teeth large and square,
your lips drawn back like a horse's,
smiling.

You tell a story
about a monk
who climbed a mountain
to a cave where a holy man
sat, meditating, like stone,
until the monk cut off his own arm,

threw it in the white snow,
and so the holy man became his teacher.
You say writing is like that.

For me, it's more like rain on the desert,
the turpentine smell of creosote bushes
and water running in washes that were dry,
and sometimes floods,
the water spilling over Lobo Way.
I stop, wonder at the depth,
think of the dead-end behind me
and of home across the sudden river.

W-O-U-N-D AS IN GUNSHOT

A metal mesh protected the windows and my classroom door was always locked. Dark gray shades unevenly kept out the sun. The near view was desolate: unkept dryness from the drought spread through vacant lots; newspapers and other scraps blew freely until caught in some high weeds. There was only one house, a large red-peeled frame whose owner tamed the overgrowth with geraniums planted in rows of painted tires placed around the strawlike grass and growing despite it all. In the distance stood the Sears Tower.

It was very hot. The fire hydrant gushed a flow five feet high, flooding the street and blinding the drivers trying to get through. A crowd of little children gathered, waiting to jump on the paused cars and ride screaming through the cool spray. Their dark bodies shone on the hood, on the roof. They held tight on the bumper, on the trunk, then jumped down, squealing, while the stunned driver sped off.

The older kids were coming now, mainly strolling in small groups. Few walked alone and those who did kept looking behind them, checking; and in back loomed the projects, long, tall rows of concrete riddled with dark windows. Be cautious, kids always said, and I was. They taught me that. Attendance would be low again today—heat and the end of the year—but I was still looking for three who took the same route daily: Andre, Didi, and Darnell; brother, sister, brother; Darnell always last, always straight and slow. Andre was the lookout; Darnell the one to take care of the trouble. But they hadn't made the walk to school for three mornings. I would have to call.

I had called before. The week the plays were due for competition, I asked Darnell for his number in case I needed to check anything in the script while typing.

"What do you mean by that?" he questioned.

"I mean I might not be able to read something," I said.

"You mean you want to talk to my grandmother, don't you?" he said.

"No, Darnell, I want to talk to you."

"You're trippin'," he laughed but gave me the number: 529-4321.

It wasn't always like that, being able to talk. At first he was silent. I noticed only his eyes, large and waiting to see if anyone would answer, or cast down to his desk, not wanting to be recognized. When we wrote in journals, he used the paper from my desk and wrote only a little, at the top, in small print so that it was the blankness of the page that was most striking. His ideas were brief: "Somedays I hate not fighting or hurting"; or "I had a friend once. I have a memory of it. It is a sad feeling, but I'll live"; or "This week-end I'm going to have sex and get a notebook."

There wasn't much to write back, only to say, "Keep writing" or "Tell me more" or "Did you get the notebook?" One Monday he came in and stood at my desk and just looked for a moment.

"My grandmother says blue eyes like yours glow in the dark." After he finished a sentence, he held two fingers at the corner of his mouth as if that were his control, the way to keep his insides in.

The others were watching, waiting for an answer. He wasn't kidding; they weren't laughing.

"She said at night that you can see them glowing. When you sit up and open your eyes, they cut through the dark," and his eyes were steady and deep and brown.

I couldn't help smiling at the thought of this image so I opened my eyes wide and said in a low voice, "They do."

He smiled a bit and sat down.

It was later that he really began to write, bringing with him a folded pad and short pencils. Journal writing grew into dreams of owning a McDonald's and flying to Florida, and he began to color his past and put it on the page. He brought it all to his play, "Caring," and his character, Big T.

"Big T's a good name," I told him.

"Why do you think I picked it," he said.

"What's he going to do?" I asked.

"I'll tell you what he's not going to do," he told me. "He's not gonna go to no blackboard to fool with words that he can't understand. No, he's not gonna waste his time lookin' stupid for no one."

"So what's going to happen?" I asked.

"He'll fight with the teacher. But the teacher'll be crazy and get on him to come to school early. Learn to read better, he'll say, but Big T won't be so sure about that. He'll come early all right, but he'll be smoking a joint in the john with his boys."

"So, then what?"

"So, I'll get up to there and then see."

I watched him work, carefully, slowly, as if each word were a story. His red pants were pressed to a shine. The seams were sewn in thick white thread, and I wondered about this boy wearing clothes burst from the growing of somebody else and now tightly darned for him; and I wondered about the hands that sewed those seams. I never met his mother, but his grandmother came for grades and she told me to watch him. She said that things were fine now but. . . . She looked at his report card with pride and he nodded, standing there letting her talk to me; I had an image of his smiling so broadly that his face was all smile and brightness, yet he really barely moved his lips. She seemed to know though: there was a bond between them that was tight and invisible. She gave him a sidelong glance and said, "Watch him now, he's been stubborn at times."

I wondered if it were her hands that injected pride each time they found a broken stitch and she wished she could be designing anything else for him instead of fixing seams. He was her boy, and then she jabbed that needle sharp as ice in line. Injecting pride. Maybe it was that which made Darnell hesitate sometimes, look at his words, then stop, stretch long legs forward until the seams tensed, and set a cold face: no more writing today. He wouldn't look the fool for anyone. He'd think on it and work tomorrow. He always did.

"The teacher almost gives up," Darnell said. "He pulled him out of the john and was hollering like wild."

"But what are they saying?" I asked. "It's important to work on the dialogue; how they talk to each other."

"I don't need to work on it," he stated. "The teacher says, 'Big T, you don't want to learn anything. You only want to run in gangs, snatch purses, and kill old folks.' And Big T says back, sorta soft and steady, 'Don't start talking. Don't even try. You don't know me. You don't know nothin' about me.' "

I looked at him and thought, What do I know? What do I know of this boy Darnell, with his deep brown eyes, saying in his play, "You don't know me. Don't even try." When we read the plays aloud to the others, they nodded at these lines and said, "That's straight. Yeah, that's straight."

And I guess it was straight but all I really knew was that Darnell kept on trying to finish his story and that seemed enough.

"I figure it all works out in the end," he said. "Big T learns to read, graduates with honors, lands a job and gets a girl."

"That's impossible in just a few pages," I laughed.

"It can happen," he said seriously.

"What makes the change?" I asked.

"His friend dies," he said.

"Show me," I told him and we went back to the death scene. It was only a few lines and I asked him if he thought that was enough.

"It doesn't take long," he said.

"But how would this be staged?" I asked. I was worried about development and props and effect.

"Some kind of blur," he said, waving his hand back and forth. "And sound. That's important. Loud, loud sounds that you know he'll hear forever."

"Who will hear?" I asked.

"Big T," he said loudly like I should have known. "The boy Big T who's kneeling there when his friend dies, who can't drag him away and can't make it stop. That's the one who'll hear and he can just stay there, Big T, kneeling. Maybe he can put his hands on his ears, or maybe he can put his head on his friend's chest and say, 'Come on, Juice. You'll make it through. You can't die, Juice. You can't die.'"

"His name was Juice?" I asked.

"His name was Juice," he answered.

"You can put all this in the scene," I told him softly.

"It won't all fit," he said.

Then he continued to work, and I moved on; but I didn't know how deep he was reaching, I didn't know what all this would show. I was thinking of a play and how we could stage it; he was thinking of a life already staged and he began to shout at Lashon, who was sitting beside him.

"Stop acting stupid, Shon, and look at this." He held out a sheet from his pad that had words written and crossed out and written again: w-o-o-n-d and w-o-u-n-d and w-u-n-d. He pointed to one and said, "Is this how you spell it, Shon? Now don't be playin' with me."

And Shon said, "I don't know what the fuck you're talking about, Darnell! What's a wund?"

And Darnell stood up with flashing eyes, with a tall broad strength and hard, torn voice and he pulled up his shirt and pointed to a scar jagged on his side and he said, "I mean wound like in gunshot, like in gunshot, Shon!"

We all sat silent and I finally said, "Wound . . . W-O-U-N-D."

"Thank you," he said and sat down.

I think of Darnell and I think of his play and how he made life so fine on the page and I wonder when he's going to come back to school; when he'll walk here again in that straight line: brother, sister, brother; he watching in back. And I want to see him and I want to call him and hear his voice say, "Yeah, this is Darnell. . . . Sure, I'll be back. . . . It's just something here that needs some tendin', but then I'll be back. . . . Yeah, yeah, I hear ya' . . . I'll be back. . . ."

But I'm afraid to make the call. Afraid of what I don't know. Worried and afraid that one of those windows in one of the buildings that loom in the distance has for some reason really gone dark; that he's not coming back, that he won't be walking in a straight line, cutting a path through the dry vacant lots past the tires with geraniums to this shadowy room; that when I dial his number like so many others I've dialed, I will hear a bodiless voice intoning again and again: "529-4321 . . . That number has been disconnected. There is nothing more known about 529-4321. . . ." And this will be no play: this will just be an end.

ELEVEN IS TOO YOUNG
TO DIE

LISA NOBLE

When Justin died,
after he jumped off the bus and ran smack in front of a
    milk truck
looking left but not right,
I didn't congratulate myself on living
or wish that I had gone instead of him.
I didn't replay his death in my mind over and over
as the books said I would.
Instead, I watch the classroom door expecting him to arrive
and I laugh aloud in the solemnness of the church.

These days, I panic when a school bus stops
and a car goes through the out-turned red sign.
I watch the heifers suckle their calves,
noses nuzzled under warm bellies.
And I cry when Mom cuts a daisy
for a bouquet of snow white and yellow
that I am to take to school.

I wore "Easter Sunday Best" the day of the funeral.
Black somehow didn't seem appropriate.
I sat, a wilting flower among the coal.
And when a child broke down and sobbed
in Justin's father's arms,
I ran
because that was all I could think to do.

RECEIVING A RIVER

RICHARD L. HAVENGA

*O*utside my window a tall tower stretches skyward. Stiff, erect, cold steel, anchored with taut wires from many directions. This antenna catches invisible signals and translates them into pictures and sounds. When I'm outdoors, I'm an antenna. More like an insect's antennae, more flexible, and open to sensory signals.

I've been hearing strong signals from rivers this year and followed the call to learn what I could, to discover what rivers had to offer. I discovered that the spirit of the river is given freely to those who receive it.

Boardman River

Swift, flat surface
rich in texture.
Your water wrinkles.
Fluid,
folding upon yourself
while flowing.

Like lines on topographic maps,
curving while parallel,
edge over edge
water upon water.
Forming, re-forming.
Appearing, disappearing.

Reappearing.
Magic water.
Art in motion,

swirling with poetry
gliding among the Alders
like time flowing forward.

Honey Creek

It's early December, an early Saturday morning, and I'm cross-country skiing along Honey Creek. Rock filled, shallow, and gravel bottomed, this creek washes loud with current.

Overnight, the first major snowfall of the season, a four-to-five-incher, has highlighted the darkness of the water. A black snake crawling through the white landscape. This climax forest is muffled by the insulating snow, amplifying the liquid music from the creek. Snow-mounded boulders bulge above the rushing current like winter turtles frozen in midstream.

The sun is breaking through retreating clouds and streaming through the narrow opening the creek creates in the canopy of mature oaks. I stop in the middle of the plank bridge. I lean on the rail and face upstream, face the wind, face the wide creek coming at me.

The stream, it seems, is my future coming at me. From a distance it's only a band of water sloping toward me. The closer it comes, the better I can see the ripples, eddies, swirls, and bubbles. Only the present is clear.

Like time, the current tumbles toward me, slides under the bridge, and rushes downstream. The stream is one body, a long fluid ribbon from beginning to end, yet I can observe only this one part, can live only this present moment.

It's hard to leave this spot. Months from now I'll be walking on these ski trails along the creek banks. The snow will melt, buttercups will emerge, and frogs will climb up groggy from the winter mud to claim this stretch of creek. The seasons will flow on.

Flat River

Wide and shallow, I'm wading knee-deep, though cautiously, along the wild banks of the Flat River. Long, ribbony leaves of aquatic plants flex and sway, undulating with the sweep of current. Like the hair of an underwater maiden, green strands tangle and tickle my legs. I touch my palm flat to the water's surface, believing I can feel the pulse of the river.

The afternoon sun warms a line of turtles balanced on a narrow log.

A great blue heron glides gently downriver, landing silently on an inside bend where the stones collect and pile deep enough to shallow the water. He stalks in frozen motion, staring between the stones for prey.

Reading a River
(Great Blue Heron)

Wading
on legs
yellow scaled
stiff as sticks.

Reaching
with neck
gray feathered
supple as a snake.

Staring
through eyes
stone hard
fixed as the stars.

I'm beginning to learn how to receive a river: stay long enough. Place myself like an alder leaning from the bank, like a boulder in midstream, like a heron silent in the shallows. Listen to the current to learn the language. Feel the music in its soul.

WORDS: AN EXPRESSION OF ORDER

KERRY RIDOLFI

I was a child whose best friend was a pen. A big, fat, Bic blue was my choice, and I'd spend hours alone in my room indulging my imagination, drawing and writing stories and poems. As a child I seemed to go through phases in my writing like students today go through R. L. Stine, The Sweet Valley Twins, and Lurlene McDaniel. One month I'd be writing mysteries, the next month studying and writing about animals, the next month adventure, and then on to the topic of love. "I Was a Prehistoric Teenager" was one of my favorites. Sent back in time, four twelve-year-olds—two boys, Biff and Bob, and two girls, Sally and Sue, fight Tyrannosaurus Rex and fall in love. The words I enjoyed were seldom shared with others. It didn't matter to me. I wrote to remind myself that I existed, that there was an order, despite the chaos I experienced in my own life.

I'm astonished to realize that as a child I never wrote in school; we were so busy doing worksheets and reading basals. It wasn't until eighth grade that I had a teacher who allowed us to write, and at that point writing began to take on a different shape for me. I wrote a short poem called "Rich Man, Poor Man," comparing the two. Encouraged by my teacher, who I knew loved books and words, I read my poem out loud to the class. Despite my timid voice they were moved and applauded. Out of the reading came a fiery class discussion about the issues of wealth and poverty. It was then I realized that words had power—power to make others think, power to make others feel. To me, at age fourteen, that was magic.

Today I continue to order my world through words.

King of the Playground

In hallways I avoided you
As children do
When railroad tracks
Make a difference.
Until you cornered me
Bully of the playground
Pulling down your shirt
To shock me;
Blood-crusted craters
Scattered on your back
BB pellets fired
From little distance and bragged:
"My father locks me in the freezer."
I lifted my petticoat,
Welts swelled purple
Across my skin,
To your astonished face,
I ruined the game.

The events that happen to us when we are young cannot, of course, be undone . . . but they can be controlled and managed through the power of words. I wrote "King of the Playground" when I was young; as a child I often ordered my world through words. Words helped me make sense of pain, anger, friendship, love. They were something that I had that was mine.

Writing helps young people order their world. Whether they make a joyful sound or one of disturbance, words have a way of clearing the air. Time and time again I see this in my students' writing.

Dorian is ordering her feelings about the adults around her when she writes:

In the parents' world there is
Quietness, stiffness, and work.
Their colors are only gray,
Not purple, orange, and bright green
Like in the children's world.
There are not imaginary beings,
Not merriment, and joyful noises,
Not spaceship rides to the planet Mars,
Not swinging to and fro on stars,
Not flying pigs,
Not spiked-up wigs,
Not hairy fishes
Not tons of wishes,
Not in the parent world.

T. J., whose family adopted a greyhound, is seeking order when he writes an editorial about the issue of greyhounds being euthanized. He begins:

> Each year more than 40,000 dogs are killed in this country because they are not fast enough to race. They are bred for racing, and if they cannot keep up, the tracks are forced to put them down or give them away. At home I have a greyhound. He is the most playful and lovable dog I know.

Stacey writes about a reality that too many children know in her short story called "Shattered," about a family that is coming apart:

> "I hate this family," grumbled Alisha, as she sat in her room listening to her parents arguing. They were fighting about money as usual. The tears streamed down her face like rain, she brushed them away with the back of her hand ... Lately, Alisha's parents had been fighting, actually not lately; a lot. Alisha could not understand what was happening but she knew one thing for sure, the fights were getting worse and worse.

Carissa tells me she is writing about "soft pain" when I ask her about her story of losing a friend to a horrible disease, and Laurie's story about teenagers, drugs, and AIDS reflects one adolescent's mind sorting out the realities that confront her today.

Observing a child use words to help shape his or her feelings is a powerful experience, both for me and for that child. There are days I wonder whether young students have any compassion or concern outside of themselves; then I go to their writing, where I always find some students struggling—as I had—to make sense of the world. Sean's poem, modelled after a work by Gwendolyn Brooks, is an excellent example.

Life Is for Me

Life is for me and is a
jumble
of mixed emotions,
Inside me I feel
arrows pointing in
different directions
and not knowing which
way to go.

There are roads all
around me,
Some leading to peaceful

and perfect life,
But most leading to
dead ends and detours.

I want to have peace
throughout the world.
I want to have someone
to guide us down the
roads
we take.

I do not want
homeless people
sitting on streets
and others at war.
I do not want people
to live in fear,
even in their own homes.

Life is for us,
For the poor and the
wealthy,
For the young and the old,
For the sick and the
healthy,
And for the shy and the bold.

We have the right to choose
what roads we take,
We have a right to be
free!

Sean McGrail

I still have my notebooks and journals from long ago filled
with faded scribbles: lines of poems, beginnings to novels, observations of the world around me that I add to daily. They are my
treasures. Words that will take me anywhere I want to go. Words
that remind me of the child that I was and the woman that I
have become. I will always remember my eighth-grade teacher,
who encouraged me to take a risk, to share my writing, to see
myself as a writer and discover the power of words. I would like
to think of some of my own students someday remembering me
as a lover of words and a writer who helped them explore their
own power through words, taking them anyplace they want to go.

References

Brooks, Gwendolyn. 1983. *Very Young Poets.* Chicago, IL: The David
Company.

WRITING FOR LIFE:
TEACHER AND STUDENTS

LINDA RIEF

*E*arly October in New Hampshire. On the drive to school each morning, I roll down the windows and drink in the air. It is green pear crisp.

On this particular day in one eighth-grade class, Matt signs up for a conference. He reads aloud the piece he's written. It's a poem about death, about a suicide, about a father. His words are quick and clean and simple—right to the point:

> The leaves move left and right.
> The wind blows with all its might.
> I'm riding in a car it didn't feel
> Very far because I slept.
> I wake up and get out of my bed
> With an absurd feeling of dread.
> The words my mom said,
> are etched in my head,
> Your father is dead, shot through the head.
> The leaves don't move left or right.
> The wind doesn't blow with all its might.
> Birds no longer take to flight.
> All is silent.
> All is dead.

"What a sad, terrible thing," I say. "The poem is so depressing I'm surprised you use rhyme. Rhyming poems are usually light and funny." This one's not funny, his shrug tells me.

I ask Matt where he got the idea for the poem. "Because it's true," he says. "Oh, Matt, I'm so sorry." I'm stuck for words. I buy time. I ask Matt if he'd mind reading the piece to Carol

Wilcox, a University of New Hampshire doctoral student frequently in my classroom. Matt goes over to the carpet and reads his poem to her. I watch Carol listening intently as he reads and then answers her questions.

Matt's father was older and suffered a serious back problem. Several years ago, the entire family—except his dad, who excused himself by saying he wasn't feeling good—visited relatives for Thanksgiving dinner. The next morning, Matt noticed that his dad wasn't at breakfast. Asking when his dad would be home, he heard his mother say only, "He won't . . . he's dead."

While Carol is listening to Matt, I make my rounds of the students who have signed up for conferences. Debbie reads me an excerpt about a teen-age boy, a runaway, deciding whether to stay in the cold alley filled with garbage and overflowing trash cans or to return to the family he's run away from. In real life, Debbie's seventeen-year-old brother ran away. No one has heard from him in four months. In her story, the boy decides to go home.

I welcome Sherri back to school after an extended absence. Her seven-year-old sister, Katie, had been hit and killed by a pickup truck just two weeks before, when she darted across a busy street. "I would have been back earlier," Sherri tells me, "but we got my sister's ashes yesterday."

"I'm so sorry," I say. But I wonder. How do you hold the ashes of your seven-year-old sister? Your seven-year-old daughter? Next to the teddy bear on the bed? Do you keep the nightlight on so she won't be afraid of the dark? Do you just throw away her toothbrush? How does her giggle fit into the box? How do you hold the ashes of your seven-year-old sister? I move on to the next table.

Ted, an awkward, bumbling kid who takes Ritalin to control his hyperactivity, has signed up for a conference. His writing is long, and I'm not sure I'll have time to listen to the whole piece. But when he starts reading, after telling me, "I jus' wanna know if you like it," I ask him to keep reading. The writing is fresh, vivid, filled with humorous detail. It's about a boy named Trevor who wakes up to a day when everyone likes him and has gone out of his or her way to be kind to him: the school bus driver who's making pancakes and sausage for him on a portable grill at the bus stop . . . the math teacher who gives him an engraved leather chair to sit in for his great attitude and effort during fractions . . . the dance dedicated to him for being such a well-liked, all-around great kid. When he gets to the part about a blonde, blue-eyed Swedish "babe" saving a seat for him on the bus, Ted stops, leans in, looks me straight in the eye and says, "Can I be honest with you about what would happen to a fourteen-year-old boy if this was true about the Swedish babe?"

"Of course," I say, all too quickly. Ted reads, "Trevor got a hard-on the size of Florida as he sat down next to her." How can I say, "Nice detail. I can really see it"?

In the middle of our conference the fire drill wails. Once outside, Bevin, Laurie, and Kelly discover a new kind of jewelry. They remove their earrings and plunge the stems of autumn's best through their pierced ears. At the all-clear, we return to the classroom. Everyone starts writing again. Ted continues with Trevor. Matt thinks about what he might add to his dad's suicide poem. Debbie returns to writing her runaway piece.

I look up and see an entire table of girls with leaves dangling from their ears—maple red, oak orange, and the hickory's summer squash yellow. Despite their topics, perhaps *because of* their topics, these kids bring the air of October into the classroom. It is green pear crisp.

Carol looks at me and laughs. "I'm going back to first grade, where all they write about is hearts and rainbows. Life's too tough here. . . . I thought this was the All-American town, where every kid had his own mother and father, a dog, a cat, a brother, a sister. . . . How do you do it?"

How do *I* do it? I think. How do *they* do it? Maybe this *is* the All-American town.

In *Gates of Excellence* Katherine Paterson (1981) says

> Why are we so determined to teach our children to read? So that they can read road signs? Of course. Make out a job application? Of course. Figure out the destination of the bus so that they can get to work? Of course. But don't we want far more for them than the ability to decode? Don't we want for them the life and growth and refreshment that only the full richness of our language can give? . . . [We should be reading] good or even great [books] because they make the right connections. They pull together for us a world that is falling apart. They are the words that integrate us, judge us, comfort and heal us. They are the words that . . . bring order out of chaos. (17–18)

I share Paterson's passion for reading and extend that passion to writing. Our students must be allowed their voices through writing because it helps them think and feel and play with language as they make order out of their chaotic lives: their school lives, their personal lives, and the world around them.

Ted, Matt, Debbie, and Sherrie are only four of the reasons why we should be, in the words of Don Murray, "seeking diversity" in our classrooms, "not proficient mediocrity" (Rief, 1992). Every child is unique and deserves to be valued for that uniqueness. We show our students we value them as individuals when we value their voices. And we hear their voices when we invite them to show us what they know and how they know that through their writing and reading.

Through giving kids choices as they read and write, we also teach them to take responsibility for their own learning. Rexford Brown (1991), in *Schools of Thought*, says that taking responsibility for their own learning "is the only way to get them deeply engaged and committed to their education. It is a natural way to teach responsibility and reinforce the values that undergird all natural learning: courage, honesty, persistance, and respect" (249).

We will hear the unique, honest, courageous voices of our students when they are allowed to show us what they think and know and feel. It is the kind of learning that matters. Listen to the voices that emerge when our students are reading and writing for life.

In their personal lives they suffer separation, death, peer pressure, and isolation.

Stacey writes "And I'm Not Ready":

> My mother
> talks to me
> as she's cooking
> The roast she prepares
> doesn't have its familiar smell
> Outside the snow is cold
> each flake falling like a lonely leaf
> Mom drops her head in her hands
> and I can see her reflection
> off the glassy finish of the table
> She looks
> sad
> tired
> She says I will have to be more mature
> to act older
>
> Me?
> The little girl who wears ponytails in her hair?
> The little girl who does somersaults down the hall?

The little girl who plays with dolls?
To act older?
No matter how much I try to prevent
her leaving
It's going to happen anyway

and it does

she leaves

It's like an intense wind
fiercely blowing
pushing at me
pushing the child
right out of me

and I'm not ready.

In his own chaotic world, Matt talks about peer pressure, the pressure to try smoking, chewing tobacco, and drinking, in this lead to his experience:

After you here wate I have to share I hope you don't think you read a book about a bunch of loosers or vandles its more like Adam taking the frut from the tree when the serpent tempted him that's wate happend to me the sepent being temptation exposior and curreosity. The serpent promesed Adam power I was promissed the garden of Eden that simballized popularity recanision and a little athority Adames plan basicelly back fired he lost purity and ganed shame my path wasint is esy as picking a frut off a branh like Adame did I had a long and rugh path with meny obsticles along the way.

Our students' school lives are no less chaotic. They write to understand, perhaps to protest, what it is they are being asked to learn. In their own way they ask, "What's it for?"

Jay writes "School Daze":

help
i am going to be
refracted and i can't
count a present progressive
is staring me in the face with verbs crying
to be conjugated algebraic
sentences are chasing
me as i run into a mercantilist
policy a phosphorescent light appears
in front of me trying
to help me in this mass
confusion i stare at it hoping
for enlightenment
but nothing

jumps out at me so i
run head on
into a quadratic
monomial factor a voice
out of nowhere echoes around me
"You're eighth graders now!"
then why do i feel as befuddled as ever

Abby uses writing to defend her position of not wanting to participate in the eighth-grade school play, *The Mikado,* when she writes in an excerpt of a letter to her teacher:

My instant impression of this play was that it was sexist. The female characters are portrayed as being either ugly and mean, like poor Katisha, or silly and yummy, like the three sisters, Peep-Bo, Pitti-Sing, and Yum-Yum. The male characters are equally unappealing in that they are either brutal and controlling or "dippy-do" idiots. This type of stereotypical imagery has hurt women a lot, as well as men.

I have read this play and I believe it is very degrading to the Japanese people in that there is a very narrow, simplistic portrayal of their culture. In my opinion, it does not promote a well-rounded understanding of them at all. They're not as silly and superficial as this play presents.

I am very willing to participate in a play with a socially redeeming message to the audience and a healthy balance of male and female characters. This play is extremely outdated and I find it embarrassing that we are still being entertained by this sort of silly, old-fashioned, obsolete, and, in my mind, damaging melodrama.

I think it is a violation of the first amendment of the Constitution that I have to say or sing words I do not like.

Matt also makes it clear what he thinks in response to an assigned essay:

Mr. and Miss Mcbeth
The Perfect Marige

I feed up with the hole thing how long are we going to drag this out you know we all think that Mcbeth is pond scum and Miss Mcbeth is a wench and they shuld of gone to a marige shrink long ago its apperent after reading the book waching the movies and the play we do'nt think there the worlds best cople

They attempt through writing to figure out the chaos of the world around them. They have serious issues to resolve. Jeremy worries about pollution in this excerpt from "On the Road—Summer '92":

The dunes, shadowed by scattered trees, oaks, juniper, pine, hemlock, and birch, glisten in the sunlight. Mountains of sand burn hot under my naked feet. The dunes eventually flatten out into a beach nestled near the Great Lakes.

My brother and I run up to the top of the dune and gaze out—out to see—powerplants? The powerplants of Gary, Indiana, spew their chemicals from smokestacks. The sight surprises me, like tasting brussel sprouts for the first time. I want to spit those smokestacks away. But the taste hangs in my mouth.

. . . As I lie down to sleep, I think of the millions of spots like this park that are being destroyed every day. Maybe this will be the last time I'll be able to see such blue skies, breathe such clean air, and swim in Lake Michigan. Or will the brussel sprouts ruin everything? Will the taste ever go away? . . .

Dan, in a letter to an editor, struggles with our country's role in world affairs. Why do we pay attention in one situation and not another? In an excerpt of his letter he writes:

I feel that the United States should take action against the Serbians. In Bosnia people are dying every day. If we don't act now when will someone stop the slaughter? Every day that we wait means that some more children will never laugh, smile, or play.

When Saddam Hussein invaded Kuwait we took action. We sent bombers and tanks and soldiers. Now Bosnia is being invaded; people are being herded into concentration camps. And we watch. We watch as people starve and are maimed by artillery shells.

Why do we defend one and not another? Why is one group of people more valued than the other? Or, is the difference not who they are, but what they own? Does the fact that the Kuwaitis own oil and the Bosnians don't give the Kuwaitis greater right to life? By the warped standards of the American government it does.

Emma takes an especially distressing look at what she sees happening to children in our commercial, materialistic, violent world, where adults have, in her mind, relinquished responsibility. She writes:

Little Boys aren't all made
of puppy dog tails
    and frogs and snails.
Nowadays they're made
of Ninja turtles,
    GI Joes, BB guns,
      and karate clothes.
Little Girls aren't all made
of sugar and spice
    and everything nice.

Today they're made
of street-corner Barbies,
    permanent hair
      dyes,
    skeleton earrings,
    and dark black lies.
Parents contribute
    when kids are
      young,
    giving them TVs
    and dangerous guns.
But as kids grow up
    and still
Keep these
    bad morals till
Society becomes
    a black hole
For criminals who take
    their mightly toll.
Nowadays, boys aren't
  made
    of puppy dog tails
    and frogs and snails
And girls aren't made
    of sugar and spice
    and everything nice.

And sometimes, despite all the chaos of the world around them, these young men and women figure out how, and where, real learning happens, as Trisha does in "School Days":

In Maine I've learned . . .
how to sail my grandparents' sunfish boat
the backstroke, freestyle, and the deadman's float
how to catch a pickerel on a rod and reel
and how to enjoy red hotdogs every third meal.

In Maine I've learned . . .
how to walk through a swamp, and burn off a leech
to lay in the sun or dig traps in the beach
how to dive through the water or flip from the float
to ski on one ski from my grandfather's boat.

In Maine I've learned . . .
how to steer a canoe
or if it flips, what I'm to do
how to catch a turtle with just my bare hands
or build castles and cities with water and sand.

> In Maine I've learned . . .
> to absorb what I see
> and how to relax and just be me.

Given choices, kids will read and write about things they care deeply about. *We* allow them those choices. But in Paterson's (1981) words, "We cannot give [our students] what we do not have. We cannot share what we do not care for deeply ourselves. If we prescribe books [and I would add, prescribe writing] as medicine, our children have a perfect right to refuse the nasty-tasting spoon" (17).

We cannot give our students the love of reading and writing if we ourselves are not passionate about reading and writing. All teachers should be readers and writers, but language arts teachers *must* be writers and readers. *We must be what we teach in order to*:

- recognize and understand the challenges, the frustrations, and the achievements experienced by our students;
- understand the complexity of the processes in which we ask children to participate;
- show our students that we value what we ask them to do by doing it ourselves;
- give students models of adults as lifelong learners to whom they can apprentice themselves;
- empower ourselves personally and professionally.

When Maureen Barbieri taught seventh grade in Ohio, one of her students said, "You know what I like about this class? You're *not* like the gym teacher. Like when she coaches swimming, she never gets in the pool. She never gets wet. She just stands on the side yelling, 'Go faster! Go faster!' "

We do not have to be published authors any more than that gym teacher has to be an Olympic swimmer. But we do have to "get wet" for all the reasons I listed above. "Kids copy kids," says Ted Sizer (1992) of the Coalition for Essential Schools, "but even more they copy adults. The adolescents among them are exquisitely attuned to evidence of hypocrisy; they deeply resent dicta from their elders that signal 'do what I say not what I do' " (27).

If we ask our students to keep reader's-writer's journals, we have to keep journals. If we ask our students to read and write every day, we have to read and write every day. If we ask our students to assemble portfolios, we have to assemble our own portfolios. And it is not just for all the reasons I've already mentioned. Our reading, writing, and thinking make *us* literate human beings. They give us individuality.

The most important reason to be what we teach is because reading and writing give us our own voices. *Reading and writing and speaking empower us, personally and professionally,* as we think and feel and play with language in trying to make order out of our chaotic lives. Robert Frost said the writing of each of his poems had given him "the occasion for a fresh think" (Romano, 1987, p. 25). Our students need occasions for a "fresh think," just as we do. I need to figure out what I think and know and feel. Certainly I feel good about what my students accomplish as readers and writers, but I need that sense of personal and professional satisfaction for myself as well.

So I write—with my students, at home, in restaurants, in the car, in the shower—compiling notes, observations, reactions, snatches of conversations, headlines from the paper—in journals, on napkins, on the backs of deposit slips, on grocery lists, on playbills, in my head. I have become the observer, the listener to everything around me, not knowing where or when or how these "fragments of language," as Don Murray calls them, will reappear in my text, yet always surprised when they do. I too write to make order out of my personal life, my school life, and the chaotic world around me.

A five-minute conversation at a reunion became a twenty-five-page short story. My son's comment about the purchase of his first car became the lead to a coming-of-age story: "Mom, wait'll you see the bargain I got. Why the wheels alone are worth two hundred dollars!"

At a conference Shelley Harwayne read a memoir by Eloise Greenfield entitled "Mama Sewing." In the margin of my notes I wrote "mom was a wonderful seamstress—the best—she won the sewing prize at Malden High—I saw it in her yearbook—1938." Those notes became my own memoir, working out my own guilt.

To Mom, with Love

My mother was the best seamstress at Malden High. In 1938 she won the prize in home economics—a dress mannequin, a dummy body.

When I was in seventh grade she tried to help me sew the apron I had to make in sewing class. She pulled out her White sewing machine. She filled her mouth with straight pins and patiently showed me how to lay out the tissue pattern pieces on the material.

"Watch the selvage. Keep the arrows on the tissue all running the same way.

"Make sure the pins all head in the same direction.

"Use the pinking shears so it won't ravel.

"Here's a needle. Baste the pieces together before you use the machine.

"Is your bobbin full?"

I refused to baste. "I just wanna stitch it," I whined, impatient to get started, impatient to finish. With the first mistake I ripped the apron from the needle. "This is dumb," I said, and threw the paisley pieces to the floor.

Mom died in September 1985. I never told her how sophisticated I felt in that backless, satin prom dress. I forgot to say thank you for the elegant, lace-trimmed wedding gown. She never heard me say how cute her grandsons were in those tailored Easter suits.

I wish I could tell her how warm and comfy we all are through cold New Hampshire winters under those hand-stitched quilts. I wish I could tell her how often neighbors ask, "Who's your decorator?" as they run hands over couch cushions, upholstered chairs, pillows, and customs drapes. "My mom made them," I say.

I wish I could tell her it wasn't dumb. I think she knew. At the bottom of my quilt I run my fingers across her hand-stitched words: "June 1985—Made with love from Mom, especially for you."

I am an observer in my own classroom, jotting down what the students say and do that intrigues me. One day Mike left me the note shown in Figure 1.

Four months later I wrote in my journal:

Sept. 3rd:

Mike Z. died yesterday. Biking home from school. First day sophomore year. Hit by a truck. I cried in class today. Mike was my student in 7th grade—an awkward, gawky kid who had a hard time making friends. Found friends in his reading. Created friends through his writing. He visited me often through 8th and 9th grade. Brought me writing to respond to. Books he wanted me to love. All fantasy. I don't enjoy fantasy. But Mike persisted. Just before school got out last June he brought me a tape—Piers Anthony's *The Magic of Xanth*. "Listen," said Mike. "I figured it out. If you just listen to this while you're sleeping, I think you'll learn to like these books. Sorta like learning foreign languages."

I laughed—and promised again to read—and to listen. Today I look around my classroom. Mike's books sit gathering dust on top of my file cabinet. The tape? In my desk drawer with broken pencils, pen caps, white-out, and chess pieces. Michael's voice fills my room. In his writing. In his books. His tape. I listened over the years, but

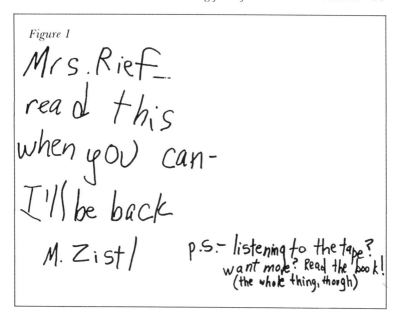

Figure 1

Mrs. Rief
read this
when you can—
I'll be back

M. Zist /

p.s.— listening to the tape?
want more? Read the book!
(the whole thing, though)

somehow I never really heard him. Now it's too late to let Mike know I cared enough to try to like fantasy, for him.

I read Mike's writing—and cry again. How many pieces of writing like "Arthur" have I read—have other students listened to—yet never really heard the writer's voice? Tonight I'll listen to *The Magic of Xanth*. For Michael.

After listening to students in my homeroom talk about what they were learning about sexuality in health seminars, I began thinking, how different it was for me in school—a *few* years back. I shaped my memories into:

Sex Education, 1956

Dressed in maroon gym suits
our initials embroidered
over the left breast pocket
we were herded like veal calves
into the darkened locker room
to see **the movie.**
Miss Coleman, the gym teacher,
fed us information
about our bodies our womanhood.
She showed us diagrams of the you-tear-us.
In the dark I couldn't see

Pam's or Anne's or Donna's face.
Did they too understand
that in a year
or two
we would bleed to death?
Our insides would fall out? even though
Miss Coleman kept saying, "It's normal, it's
natural, you'll be young ladies then."

How had my mother survived?
Why hadn't she mentioned this?
With knees pulled tightly to my chest
    I didn't feel milk-fed,
    nourished.

And I, too, am perplexed by world events. After studying
the Holocaust and World War II through literature with my
students, and after visiting the Vietnam Veterans Memorial in
Washington, D.C., I worked out my thoughts in writing, in this
lead to an eight-page essay.

Why Should We Remember?
Reflections from the Vietnam Veterans Memorial

I watch as a little boy drags his fingers across the wall, as carelessly
as Tom Sawyer thumped a stick across a white picket fence. He stares
at the names.
"These are all people killed in Vietnam?" he asks his dad.
"Yes," answers his father.
"Even the ones on that side?" he asks, sweeping his hand to the
right.
"Yes," his father says again.
He cups his hands behind his head, scans left, then right. "Why?"
he asks. "Why?"

. . . There is a guilt that drags me quickly into and out of this
foxhole of black granite. I don't read the names. I don't make eye
contact with the visitors. I don't listen to the grief.
On a park bench I distance myself from this memorial, trying to
figure out what I am doing here, why this slab of stone draws me in
again and again. Two men walk slowly past me. "What was the biggest
year?" one asks. "Oh, '68," says the second man. "I don't know the
exact count, but we lost the most in '68."
Where was I at the height of this undeclared war, in 1968? Married. Walking down maple-shaded Main Streets. Playing with babies.
Picking blueberries in New Hampshire. Eating lobsters in Maine.
Hamburgers at McDonald's. Taking hot showers. Sleeping under
down comforters. Turning doorknobs. Flipping light switches.

Drinking cold water from the tap. Complaining of the heat, of the cold, of the sun, of the rain.

TV brought Vietnam into my family-room: M-16's, machine guns, tanks; headless, limbless, napalmed bodies of Asian children and American boys; rice paddies, water buffalo, bamboo and red mud; Dak To, Quang Tri, Danang, Chu Lai. I watched protesters at home burn draft cards and American flags. Heard about draft dodgers fleeing to Canada, chewing raw coffee beans, injecting milk into their blood streams. None of it made sense to me. I turned it all off and read stories of ducklings to my sons. . . .

I need to know I am a learning, feeling, thinking, growing individual along with my students. Reading, writing, and speaking tell me *I am.* They are what make me human. They make me literate. They empower me.

By writing, we communicate what we think with many different audiences. My personal writing is for me first. If someone else is affected by that writing in any way, then I am doubly pleased. My professional writing is for me and other educators. Two recent events made me realize the importance of the professional reading, writing, and speaking of classroom teachers.

Last spring I attended a national conference. The speaker at one particular session laid out a step-by-step lesson plan that reduced a fine piece of literature to trivialized right-or-wrong answers. She had "starters" for all the writing connected to the book. She had refined the process to the degree that her plan even told other teachers when to erase the board. At the end of her presentation, she leaned into the audience and said, "And you know the best part—teachers don't even have to think." Listeners clapped. I was angry, at the speaker, at the audience, and at myself, for not jumping up and walking out.

And recently, while speaking at a conference in the midwest, I was having breakfast with an "educational consultant" who was also there to speak. He hadn't been in the classroom for years. Our discussion centered on what each of us was going to talk about. When I questioned his offerings as "prescriptive" and "formulaic," I learned very quickly what this "consultant" thought about teachers. "Face it, Linda," he said between bites of scrambled eggs, "teachers aren't too bright. They want someone to tell them what to do, when to do it, and exactly how to do it." I was outraged.

If we teachers want to be heard as professionals beyond the staff room walls, we must do more than fume and sputter about no one listening. We must risk our thoughts and feelings and

ideas by commiting them to paper. We must open the doors we
have shut on ourselves. We must read and write and speak as
professionals if we want to be heard as professionals and as
human beings.

I did not come to writing easily. I still have all the critical
analysis papers I wrote in twelfth grade for Mr. Webb: "The
Devil and Daniel Webster," "Evil in *The Scarlet Letter*." All A + 's. I
was very good at taking notes and giving all the right information
back. All Mr. Webb's. He surrounded us with language but didn't
trust us to give him any of our own. He never invited us to show
him what we were able to do with our knowledge, our language.

Don Graves invited me to speak in my voice. "Well, here we
all are," he said, as he glanced around the classroom at the
University of New Hampshire. "Let's write." This was my first
graduate course. I had taken writing courses before, but no one
had asked us to write. We had just talked about writing. But now
I was too far into the room to leave graciously. And I was sitting
next to the professor—the penalty for arriving last. Silence filled
the room. Don's pen made the only movement—the only sound.

Scratching pens and pencils began to fill the silence. I wrote
about the last thing that had happened to me, a near catastrophe
at the Durham dump. After forty minutes Don had us get into
partners and read. I was Don's partner. He not only laughed in
all the right spots but asked me to tell him more. He heard my
words. He reacted. And he wanted more.

But telling "more" is not easy. And writing honestly is down-
right hard sometimes. On Mondays I maintain a twenty-minute
silent write in each class. That is when I work on my writing,
before I move around talking with students about their writing.
I keep a reader's-writer's journal, where I do quick writes with
the students in response to something I read aloud. For example,
I read Ruth Whitman's (Mazer, 1989, p. 14) "Spring," which
begins "When I was thirteen, I believed. . . ." I asked the students
to start their response with "When I was [a certain age], I believed. . . ." In my journal I wrote:

> When I was 15 I believed the world would be destroyed by an atomic
> bomb but Debbie and Pam would probably survive because their
> fathers were rich and they had bomb shelters. I believed the most
> important thing in life was a date for the Jr. Prom, but I'd never
> have one because my nose was too long, my hair was too short, my
> legs were too fat, and I wasn't a cheerleader. I believed David loved
> Paula because she plucked her eyebrows. I believed I was poor be-

cause we had a linoleum floor and only one bathroom. Summers I worked two jobs to buy my own desk. Anne not only had a desk, but a vanity. The top opened and a mirror popped up. Anne had a flowered stool on which to sit. Donna had a summer house down the Cape. I had a fan in the bedroom window. Donna and Pam went to Russell Curry dance lessons in powder blue organdy, puffy pink taffeta. They wore white gloves and touched boys' hands. I sat in the oak tree and spied on neighbors, raked leaves on Saturday afternoons in the fall, and skated on the Hornstra's pond in winter. Donna talked of the Falmouth Playhouse in the summer, the Boston Ballet in winter, *The Nutcracker* at Christmas. I watched Little League baseball behind the junior high and saw my little sister play Mary in the Christmas creche. I ate ham and beans at the Methodist church on Saturday nights. Jan talked about New York delis and prime rib after weekend trips with her father. I never dared bring friends home when I was 13, 14, 15 . . . How would I explain Dad passed out on the living-room couch, the three weeks' beard, the smell of stale beer, scotch, cigarettes . . .

Yes, writing is difficult. My first writing was in the parent newsletter, letting parents know what the students were doing in our sixth-grade social studies class. The topic was safe. Still— what if I said something incorrectly? What if I spelled something wrong? I was more terrified of writing in that first newsletter than I am now of sharing honest thoughts and feelings in a class full of eighth graders.

What I want for my students is what I want for myself. I believe it is what we all want. We want to know that we know something. We want to communicate our ideas, our thoughts, and our feelings, for practical, purposeful, and authentic reasons. We want to play with language and find joy in learning. We want to discover our own voices. We want to laugh, cry, and make order out of our chaotic worlds. We want to develop skills as readers, writers, and speakers. We want someone to listen to us. We want our voices to be heard, both personally and professionally. We want to make a difference.

Writing *is* thinking. It is, in the words of Tom Romano (1987), "the most powerful tool" we can put in the hands of our students. It is the most powerful tool we can take up for ourselves.

If we as teachers want to be heard as professionals, we must risk our thoughts and feelings and ideas by committing them to paper.

In defining literacy, Don Graves says, "The final goal is not total mastery, but rather the lifelong wonder of learning." The most powerful message we give to our students is our own "life-long wonder of learning."

At the end of the year I ask students to include in their portfolios a one-page synthesis of what they've discovered about themselves as learners by assembling and reflecting on the contents of the portfolio. Katie's one-pager is filled with the wonder of her own learning:

> When you are a fourteen-year-old, it is often difficult to explain who you are and what your likes and dislikes are, because this is a time, at least for me, when I want to experience many different things. When I was younger, my heart was set on being a ballerina. My whole life revolved around dance for seven years. When I entered middle school, I found the need to expand my interests and set aside my toeshoes for field hockey cleats and track shoes. It was about this same time that I began to experience the power of the written word, both in the books I began to read, and in the things I began to write. I was especially inspired by the books of Maya Angelou and Bette Greene, and it was through their words that my interest in women's rights and human rights really began. My writing has become a way for me to think and discover who I am.
>
> I am a sensitive person who cares about the quality of life for others and the environment. I love the coast of Maine, where I spend my summers each year . . . the feeling of the sand between my toes and the quiet solitude of the ocean make me happy and peaceful. I am an optimist because I try to look at all possibilities, but I am a pessimist too, because my perceptions of the world around me often don't meet my expectations.
>
> Right now, I'm trying to consider my Bazooka Bubblegum fortune which said, "Your success is only limited by your desire," and I'm trying to try on as many shoes as I can to try to find the one that best fits me in life.

We need to allow ourselves this same sense of wonder. It is what gives our life meaning. It is what makes us literate. It is what gives our students' lives meaning. It is what makes them literate.

At the end of every school year I ask my students, "If you had to name the one thing I did that helped you the most this year, what would that be?" Inevitably they say, "You wrote with us and read with us." Our students watch every move we make. They know what we value by what we do.

It is no accident that the books from which I read aloud are the books students read most often: *Night, One Child, The Outsiders*. It is no accident that Lizzie reads and writes about Vietnam. It is no accident that Stacy writes about her mother or Shawn about his father.

I write about my mother-in-law escaping from Hitler in World War II. I read *Night* by Elie Wiesel and write a letter to him. It is no accident that Sandy writes about the Holocaust or that Jill writes a letter of protest and repulsion to "Hitler." It is no accident that I can see my poem "Waiting for Her to Die" in Lindsay's poem "Remembrance." When we read and write about what matters to us, students read and write about what matters to them. We are the curriculum in our own classrooms.

Who is reading and writing for? It's for our students—and us—for life. It is what makes the air in our classrooms green pear crisp.

References

Brown, Rexford. 1991. *Schools of Thought.* San Francisco, CA: Jossey-Bass.

Hayden, Torey L. 1980. *One Child.* New York: Avon.

Hinton, S. E. 1967. *The Outsiders.* New York: Dell.

Mazer, Norma Fox. 1989. *Waltzing on Water: Poetry by Women.* New York: Dell.

Paterson, Katherine. 1981. *Gates of Excellence.* New York: E. P. Dutton.

Rief, Linda. 1992. *Seeking Diversity: Language Arts with Adolescents.* Portsmouth, NH: Heinemann.

Romano, Tom. 1987. *Clearing the Way: Working With Teenage Writers.* Portsmouth, NH: Heinemann.

Sizer, Theodore R. 1992. "What's Missing." *World Monitor,* November.

Wiesel, Elie. 1960. *Night.* New York: Bantam.

CONTRIBUTORS

Maureen Barbieri has taught middle school in New Hampshire and Ohio and teaches now in South Carolina. She is an instructor in the New Hampshire Writing Program and has published articles in *English Journal, Language Arts, To Compose: Teaching Writing in Secondary School and College, Workshop 4,* and *Workshop 5.* She serves as chair of the Middle School Task Force for the National Standards Project for English Language Arts.

Mary Pierce Brosmer currently teaches full time in "Women Writing for (a) Change," a school she founded for women writers. She continues to write poetry and to explore ways of creating reading and writing communities in a variety of settings.

Linda Cunningham is Assistant Professor of Business Communication at Salt Lake Community College in Salt Lake City, Utah. She is working on her thesis for the master's degree in the Theory and Practice of Writing from Utah State University. Married 28 years to Perry Cunningham, a sociologist, they are the parents of five children (ages 13 to 25).

Richard L. Havenga teaches Reading Workshop, Writing Workshop, and Life Science to seventh graders at Crestwood Middle School in Grand Rapids, Michigan. His nonfiction, short stories, and poetry have appeared in the Peninsula Writers anthologies. He and Mary, his wife of 23 years, are the parents of Sarah and Aaron.

Marcia Howell teaches English to eighth graders at Mt. Ararat School in Topsham, Maine. She also writes for a local paper in

Portland, Maine. During the summer she is in the M.S.T. program at the University of New Hampshire.

William Johnson lives in rural Geauga County, Ohio. His recent work has appeared in the *Denver Quarterly* and *Heartlands.* He teaches at University School in Shaker Heights, Ohio.

Mary Mercer Krogness has been a full-time classroom teacher and part-time writer for the last thirty years. She has decided to write full time. She is putting the finishing touches on her book, *Just Teach Me, Mrs. K.: Talking, Reading, and Writing with Resistant Adolescent Learners* (Heinemann). She recently began writing a young adult novel and will continue writing poetry, professional articles, and essays.

Patricia McDonald-O'Brien is an elementary reading specialist in Newtown, PA. She tries to follow Donald Murray's advice, "Never a day without a line" and writes because she loves words and discovery. Writing grants her permission to wonder.

Sharon Lauer Miller teaches sixth-, seventh-, and eighth-grade English at St. Edmund's Academy in Pittsburgh, PA. She is also a fellow of the National Writing Project and a member of the Teachers' Advisory Board for The International Poetry Forum.

Jacqueline Murphy is the Curriculum Coordinator of the Drop Out Prevention Program at Chicago Teachers' Center, Northeastern Illinois University. She is working on a manuscript that documents the methods and tells the stories of this program through the process of playwriting and improvisation in the Chicago Public Schools. She also directs a neighborhood arts partnership and teaches in its pilot program to integrate the arts into the daily curriculum of grades six through nine.

Lisa Noble just completed her first year of teaching writing at Jessamine County Middle School in Nicholasville, Kentucky. She has published in various community publications and in Donald Graves' *Explore Poetry* (Heinemann, 1992).

Ellen Rennard moved from St. Louis, Missouri, to New Mexico, where she teaches eighth- and ninth-grade English at Albuquerque Academy. Most recently she wrote a series of short poems in black marker on the sides of cardboard boxes: "Rennard, Kitchen, Fragile" and "Rennard, Living Room." She hopes never to write such poems again.

Kerry Ridolfi teaches at Hampton Academy Junior High in Hampton, New Hampshire. Between the demands of her teaching career and her commitment to cycling, she writes poetry and stories about her four-legged family. She continues to work hard at being a wordsmith.

Linda Rief teaches seventh- and eighth-grade Language Arts at Oyster River Middle School in Durham, New Hampshire. She is the author of *Seeking Diversity: Language Arts with Adolescents* (Heinemann), articles in *Language Arts, English Journal, Educational Leadership*, and chapters in *Breaking Ground, Workshop 1*, and *Workshop 2* (all Heinemann). She is an instructor in the University of New Hampshire's Summer Writing and Reading Program.

Lisa Siemens is a second-grade teacher at Sister MacNamara School in Winnipeg, Manitoba. During the two short months of summer she tries to live the "writing life," but the "teaching life" is never far away. She is a member of the Child-Centered Experience-Based Learning Group (C.E.L.) and has conducted reading and writing workshops with teachers both locally and nationally.

Lawrence Sipe has taught kindergarten through eighth grade. As the coordinator of Language Arts for the last thirteen years on a small Newfoundland school board, he was responsible for teacher inservice and curriculum and policy development. He is currently a doctoral student at Ohio State University.

Michael Steinberg teaches Freshman Writing and English Education at Michigan State University. He has published books and articles on writing and teaching, as well as stories, memoirs, poems, and plays. He is a teaching/writing consultant in the Michigan Public Schools and a cofounder of the Traverse Bay [Michigan] Summer Writing Workshops for Teachers.

CALL FOR MANUSCRIPTS

*W*orkshop 7 will be devoted to the theme **What Do We Value?** With the nation's attention turning to the establishment of standards for all students, the question seems particularly relevant.

Students and teachers in schools across the country are discovering new and effective ways of evaluating language arts learning. Self-assessment has become a part of classroom life, as students demonstrate awareness of their own strengths and needs as learners. Three-way conferences invite parents to become partners with teachers and students, articulating what it is they value in their children's learning, both in and out of school. Portfolios—in all their shapes, sizes, and designs—enable students to reflect on their growth as readers, writers, speakers, and listeners and, in some cases, to integrate other disciplines into their language arts learning.

Workshop 7 will explore these and other developments in evaluation. We invite you to send manuscripts on a wide variety of topics on this theme. Here are a few possibilities, but do not limit yourself to these:

• How has the current research on evaluation affected classroom practice?
• How can evaluation be part of learning?
• Whose values count in the classroom—students', peers', teacher's, administrators', parents', community's, the English teaching profession's? Why? How is this manifested?

- How do we communicate what we value in reading, writing, speaking, and listening to our students? Are our evaluation systems explicit or mysterious?
- How do we make evaluation an ongoing process throughout the school year?
- In what ways do we honor multiple intelligences in our evaluation processes?
- In what ways do we honor cultural diversity in our evaluation processes?
- How do we handle the dual roles of teacher and evaluator?
- Can evaluation hinder learning? What can we do about that?
- How are teachers dealing with the plethora of standardized tests imposed by districts or states?
- What are some of the possibilities portfolios offer students, parents, and teachers?
- How have parent-teacher conferences changed to accommodate new evaluation policies?
- In what ways do we evaluate our own growth as teachers? As readers and writers?
- What new systems of evaluating faculty have proven useful to teachers?

The deadline for *Workshop 7: What Do We Value?* is September 1, 1994. Follow the manuscript specifications outlined below, and send two copies of the manuscript to one of the editors at the following address:

Maureen E. Barbieri   Linda Rief
1030 Parkins Mill Road   23 Edgerly-Garrison Road
Greenville, SC 29607   Durham, NH 03824

The theme for *Workshop 8* will be **Meeting the Challenges**. Teachers often tell us that, while they are intrigued with journal articles describing current theory and practice, they do not recognize themselves, their students, or their teaching contexts in the literature. These are teachers of students for whom the system does not always work well, students who may face uncertainties at home, or who may have cognitive, emotional, or behavioral issues that make learning difficult. Sometimes these students appear apathetic, alienated, or resistant. For them, some of our current approaches to literacy instruction may need to be modified, refined, or expanded upon; they may need more structure, more direct instruction, more cohesiveness in the classroom.

Workshop 8 will bring to light teachers' attempts to reach out to such students. We hope to present a rich mosaic of classroom contexts where teachers rely on both traditional and innovative approaches to enliven learning and deepen understanding. We are eager to hear from teachers who recognize their students' strengths as well as their needs and who strive every day to find ways to build on these strengths. We invite you to consider the following questions as you generate others of your own:

- In what ways do we make our classrooms safe, structured, and secure for all learners?
- How do we build on the strengths of students who have been labeled in the past "special needs children" or "students at risk"?
- How do we balance our commitment to the entire group with our concern for the isolated, disinterested student?
- In what ways are we able to provide more direct instruction to students who seem to need it?
- How do resource room or special education teachers adapt current theory and practice to foster language and literacy learning in their own teaching contexts?
- When children appear frightened, alienated, or angry, how can we enable them to be part of the classroom community?
- What can we learn from children who seem resistant? What is the nature of their resistance? Does resistance serve them in ways that we need to understand and build on?
- How do we provide fundamentals of good language arts instruction to all children, no matter what their abilities or inclinations may be?
- To what extent do we involve parents and other community members in the life of the school to promote literacy for all?
- How do we work with other professionals—reading specialists, classroom aides, and librarians, for example—to foster literacy development? How can teachers support one another in their commitment that all children will learn?
- How are we coping with failure? Every teacher must face the heartbreak of not being able to reach a student. What do we learn from these experiences, and where do we go from there?

The deadline for *Workshop 8: Meeting the Challenges* will be May 15, 1995. Please follow the manuscript specifications outlined below, and send two copies of your double-spaced manuscript to one of the following editors:

Maureen E. Barbieri
1030 Parkins Mill Road
Greenville, SC 29607

Carol Tateishi
The Bay Area Writing Project
School of Education
University of California
Berkeley, CA 94720

Manuscript Specifications for Workshop

When preparing a manuscript for submission to *Workshop*, please follow these guidelines:

- Contributors must be teachers of grades K–8, and submissions should be written in an active, first-person voice ("I").
- Contributions should reflect new thinking and/or practice, rather than replicate the published works of other teacher-researchers.
- Submissions must adhere to a length limit of 4,400 words per article (approximately 12½ pages typed double-spaced, including illustrations and references).
- *Everything* in the manuscript must be typed double-spaced, including block quotations and bibliographies.
- References should be cited according to the author-date system as outlined in *The Chicago Manual of Style*.
- Graphics accompanying manuscripts must be camera ready.
- Title pages should include address and phone numbers.
- Manuscript pages should be numbered consecutively.
- Include a cover letter indicating the contributor's school address, home address, home phone number, and grade level(s).
- Enclose a stamped, self-addressed manila envelope so the manuscript can be returned, either for revision or for submission elsewhere.
- If the manuscript is accepted for publication, the author will be required to secure written permission from each student whose work is excerpted.

This call for manuscripts may be photocopied for distribution to classroom teachers. The editors invite all interested teachers of grades K–8 to consider sharing discoveries about teaching and learning in the pages of *Workshop*.

ABOUT WORKSHOPS
1, 2, 3, 4, and 5

W*orkshop* is an annual written by and for teachers of grades K–8, a place for teachers to share their new practices and their students' responses. The contributors are experienced teacher-researchers who avoid gimmicks and prescriptions in order to focus on how students learn the language arts and what teachers can do to help. Each *Workshop* addresses a current topic in the teaching of reading and writing. Each volume also features a discussion between an expert teacher and a professional leader, an article by a writer of children's books, and an interview with another children's author.

Workshop 1

The theme of *Workshop 1* is Writing and Literature. Its authors examine what is possible when teachers who understand real reading and writing bring them together so that students can engage in and enjoy both, draw naturally and purposefully on their knowledge of both, and discover what the authors and readers of a variety of genres actually do. A wealth of children's literature plays an essential role in their K–8 classrooms.

Readers will learn exciting new approaches to the teaching of writing and reading from teachers who understand both processes from the inside.

Contents: About *Workshop 1 Nancie Atwell* Seeking Diversity: Reading and Writing from the Middle to the Edge *Linda Rief* Casey and Vera B. *Barbara Q. Faust* An Author's Perspective:

109

Letters from Readers *Ann M. Martin*   P. S. My Real Name Is Kirstin *Daniel Meier*   The Teacher Interview: Jack Wilde *An Interview by Thomas Newkirk*   When Literature and Writing Meet *Donna Skolnick*   A Garden of Poets *Cora Five*   Everyday Poets: Recognizing Poetry in Prose *Marna Bunce*   From Personal Narrative to Fiction *Kathleen A. Moore*   Historical Fiction: The Tie That Binds Reading, Writing, and Social Studies *Patricia E. Greeley*   We Built a Wall *Carol S. Avery*   Fossil Hunters: Relating Reading, Writing, and Science *Rena Quiroz Moore*   The Author Interview: Carol and Donald Carrick *An Interview by Mary Ellen Giacobbe*   One of Us *Carol J. Brennan*   Process and Empowerment *Karen Weinhold*

Workshop 2

The theme of *Workshop 2* is Beyond the Basal. Although there is a definite movement toward new approaches to teaching reading, basal series are still dominant, and teachers who venture beyond them are in the minority. This book is directed to teachers who want to implement a literature-based curriculum and have questions about organizing a classroom that is not dependent on the structure created by a basal program.

The contributors to *Workshop 2* are teachers who have found practical, rewarding, and effective ways to move beyond basals and to make literature, students' responses to literature, and their own knowledge the heart of reading instruction. Readers, regardless of their experience, will be encouraged to bring literature into their students' lives.

Contents: About *Workshop 2 Nancie Atwell*   Stephen and *The Haunted House: A Love Story Barbara Q. Faust*   An Author's Perspective: The Room in Which Van Gogh Lived *Cynthia Rylant*   Nebuchadnezzar Meets Dick and Jane: A Reader's Memoir *Ginny Seabrook*   The Silences Between the Leaves *Marni Schwartz*   Responding to the Call *Kathy Matthews*   Once upon a Time in Room Seven *Kathleen A. Moore*   The Author Interview: Jack Prelutsky *An Interview by Kathy Hershey*   Audience: Key to Writing About Reading *Cyrene Wells*   Talk: Responding to Books the Collaborative Way *Adele Fiderer*   The Teacher Interview: Carol Avery *An Interview by Jane Hansen*   Children as Authorities on Their Own Reading *Bobbi Fisher*   Writing and Reading Literature in a Second Language *Dorothy M. Taylor*   Beyond Labels: Toward a Reading Program for All Students *Joan Levy and Rena Moore*   Apprenticeship: At Four or Fourteen *Linda Rief*

Workshop 3

The theme of *Workshop 3* is The Politics of Process. The authors describe the efforts of teachers and administrators who have engaged in the politics of process in order to teach writing and reading as they believe they should. They have joined forces with like-minded colleagues, invited dialogue with administrators, created opportunities for parents to see their children's school experience with new eyes, developed appropriate methods of evaluating literacy, and made the community part of their responsibility as teachers.

This volume is a practical invitation to teachers and administrators who are seeking strategies that will help them gain acceptance for process approaches to writing and reading in their schools.

Contents: About *Workshop 3 Nancie Atwell* An Invitation to Bake Bread *Linda Hazard Hughs* A Letter to Parents About Invented Spelling *Mary Ellen Giacobbe* An Author's Perspective: The Koala as a Teacher of Reading *Mem Fox* Portfolios Across the Curriculum *Mark Milliken* Evaluation: What's Really Going On? *Lynn Parsons* A Guest Essay: The Middle Class and the Problem of Pleasure *Thomas Newkirk* Setting the Stage *Mimi DeRose* The Teacher Interview: Toby Kahn Curry and Debra Goodman *An Interview by Yetta Goodman with Commentary by Ken Goodman* The Sun Does Not Set in Ganado: Building Bridges to Literacy on the Navajo Reservation *Sigmund A. Boloz* A Guest Essay: Learning Literacy Lessons *Patrick Shannon* "Change the Word Screw on Page 42" *Ed Kenney* Publishing and the Risk of Failure *Marguerite Graham* The Author Interview: Bill Martin, Jr. *An Interview by Ralph Fletcher* On Becoming an Exemplary Teacher: Having Dinner with Carol *Margaret Lally Queenan*

Workshop 4

The theme of *Workshop 4* is the issue of teacher research in the language arts.

Contributors examine topics like writing development, collaboration in the classroom, self-assessment, and extending the range of student writing. Several authors investigate in their essays the ways teachers describe their classrooms, both what teachers include in their stories and what they omit.

Contents: About *Workshop 4 Thomas Newkirk. Research as Storytell-*

ing: Teacher-Researcher-Storyteller *T. Gillespie* Silences in Our Teaching Stories—What Do We Leave Out and Why? *T. Newkirk* The Ethics of Our Work in Teacher-research *P. Johnson. Research as Reflection and Observation:* In Regie's Garden: An Interview with Regie Routman *M. Barbieri* Curiosity in the Classroom *B. Gravelle* Dreaming Away: Adventures in Non-Fiction *T. Hillmer* Neverending Exposition *S. Raivio* Ask Them *K. Moore* "This Fish Is So Strange To Me": The Use of the Science Journal *B. Rynerson. Research as Collaboration and Coteaching:* Academic Learning and Bonding: The Three-Year Classroom *V. Swartz* Partnership in Process: Strengthening the Teacher-Learner-School Triangle *R. Levi & G. Wood* Children Helping Children: A Cross-Grade Reading and Writing Program for Chapter 1 Students *S. Haertel. Research as Art—Art as Resarch:* Author Interview: Jean Craighead George *L. Lenz* Daffodils in Manhattan *K. Ernst* How Poems Think *D. Murray* Author Interview: Barbara Cooney *S. Stires*

Workshop 5

The theme of *Workshop 5* is the Writing Process Revisited. Celebrating the tenth anniversary of Donald Graves' profoundly influential *Writing: Teachers and Children at Work* (Heinemann, 1983), *Workshop 5* marks this decade of innovation with a reexamination of the writing process movement, for just as writing is open to revisions, so is the process of teaching writing.

This volume begins with a wide-ranging and candid interview with Graves in which he explores changes in his own thinking and the autobiographical roots of his theories. In the chapters that follow teachers provide personal accounts detailing extensions of the teaching model Graves put forward a decade ago, exploring the use of portfolios, writing about reading, and writing and the arts.

Contents: About *Workshop 5 Thomas Newkirk Interview:* The View from the Mountains: A Morning with Donald Graves *Thomas Newkirk. The Teacher as Writer:* Writing "Sanctuary" *Teresa Butchko* Stonewounds *Anne-Marie Omen* Insights into Composing the Poem "Word Raft" *Sherry Falco. The Struggle to Change:* Bridging the Grand Canyon *Vicki Swartz* My Class *Kathleen Mahan Interview:* Crossing Boundaries: Un-Silencing a Dialogue *JoAnne Portalupi Curtis, Dawn Harris-Martine, and Isoke Nia. New Questions/New Directions:* How Portfolios Empower Teaching and

Learning *Sherry Seale Swain*   Learning Good Lessons: Young Readers Respond to Books *Barbara Bagge-Rynerson*   Kristen's Story: A Moral Voice Emerges *Maureen Barbieri.*   *Writing and the Arts:* "Any Comments or Questions?" (On Recognizing a Good Story Play and Writing One) *Mona Halaby*   Strengthening Children's Literary Voices: Opera in the Classroom *Sharon Blecher and Kathy Jaffe*   From Writers' Workshop to Artists' Workshop: Expanding Meaning Through Words and Pictures *Karen Ernst* The Mind's Ear *Lisa Lenz*   The Seasons: A Year of Writing, Art, and Music *Katherine Doak Link*   Writing Class as Medicine Wheel: Paul's Story *Margaret M. Voss*